COLD WAR DIPLOMAT

Inside U.S. Diplomacy

1981-2011

COLD WAR DIPLOMAT

Inside U.S. Diplomacy

GEORGE A. GLASS

Printed in the United States of America

CWD
www.coldwardiplomat.com

First Printing

ISBN 978-0-9863463-1-6

First Edition

*To my parents, Arthur & Mildred Glass,
who stoicly backed every journey into the
distant unknown, bestowed by fate on
their only son.*

CONTENTS

PREFACE

Descriptions of diplomacy often become little more than historic recantations of detailed events. They seem to often overlook the individual moments of fear, embarrassment, or personal challenge that accompany them. In the following pages, I attempt to present personal reflections on the poignant and memorable anecdotes and events over the course of a 31-year diplomatic career in the U.S. Foreign Service, without rehashing the long history that provided the foundation for each tour of duty.

If nothing else, the intent was to answer the question of how I spent my time and what I was thinking at the time. Curiosity about what diplomats actually do is abundant. No diplomat answers the question the same way, as each diplomat collects different experiences in different countries. As my career developed, each tour appeared to me as a chapter of a book that gained pages with each day. Still, a good number of my colleagues have reflected to me their own sense of having done little of any note during their careers. This has always surprised me. The pages that follow do not generally reflect nail-biting diplomacy at the highest levels of government; rather, they seek to provide a portrait of some of the modest, yet not insignificant aspects to representing the United States abroad.

It was never my goal to be a diplomat in life. I never antici-pated passing the challenging Foreign Service exam. By the time I passed the exam and was offered a position, I was well on my way to obtaining a PhD and had funding for extensive research. I turned that aside for the Foreign Service. I would do the same again. It was, if nothing else, a diverse and sometimes exciting adventure. It also was replete with innumerable and unexpected pitfalls, into which fell many of my colleagues. Many of those pitfalls had to do with integrity and honesty; but just as many had to do with crass politics and unbridled ambitions.

I wish to acknowledge the unending support through my entire career of John C. Kornblum, my closest mentor and confi-dant. He was the most magnificent and visionary practitioner and teacher of diplomacy during my generation. I would also like to thank E. Anthony Wayne, one of the most savvy, effective leaders to be found; and Anna Borg, who understood people and govern-ment better than all others. Arthur Hartman was a towering giant to all of us. I have been honored to walk a ways with each of these extraordinary individuals.

I wish to thank my wife, Karin, and my children, Nicole and Michael, for their undying understanding and support through all the years I was distracted from them while I was working to advance the interests of the country I love. In the end, family mattered most, but I was always honored to have had the diplo-matic opportunities presented.

The opinions and characterizations are those of the author and do not necessarily represent those of the United States Govern-ment.

George A. Glass
Garmisch-Partenkirchen
December 2014

CHAPTER ONE

NEW JERSEY: EARLY YEARS

(1969)

I am often asked how one becomes a diplomat. In my case, the road to diplomatic life was completely unplanned. I had never imagined myself among the suave, glib, multi-lingual gregarious characters who occupy the focal point of cocktail parties and negotiations. In fact, my earliest psychological predisposition entailed a deep-seated fear of engaging in groups of people at all.

Elementary school had me clinging to seats in the absolute back row of every classroom, thoroughly uncomfortable with attention or being called on to speak. I was the epitome of shyness and quiet. I had few friends in school, but there were several neighbors' kids with whom I played as a child on Colfax Road, in Havertown, Pennsylvania. In those days I wanted to be a farmer.

My biological father left my mother and me when I was two, a dramatic event that has remained with me. We never saw him again. When I was seven years old my mother remarried, and my new father adopted me. We moved to Glassboro, New Jersey, and pursued typical middle-class suburban lives. Glassboro was a quiet town of about 10,000 at the time. It had farming fields in most directions, plus several small factories. My adoptive father commuted to Mobil Oil in Philadelphia each day, where he worked as an accountant for 41 years. My mother was at home, and became very active in the Presbyterian Church. I remained an only child.

I was never interested in history or politics while growing up. Yet in November 1963 my natural grandfather referred to me in a letter to my mother as a "a boy studying history." I never heard from him again and he died several months later, so I never understood what he meant, particularly as I was certainly not interested in history back then. I was drawn more to the Beatles, music, and girls. However, my adoptive father was active in politics. I recall standing with him in front of my black and white television set during the Cuban missile crisis. His utterances about the end of the world seemed out of touch to me. I recalled clearly the earlier launch of Sputnik, and the later assassination of Kennedy—the true earthquakes of the times. The Soviet Union increasingly came into focus as I approached high school.

Although I was somewhat talented academically, the public schools were quite limited in scope. And my quiet nature was always a barrier. As I started high school, I became intent on studying law. Then, as now, it seemed that the only two honorable, and well-paid, professions were law and medicine, and I could not stand the sight of blood. So I did what was expected and started studying Latin in ninth grade while most other boys took auto mechanics and shop. Teachers told me that this was what the serious students did. By tenth grade I added German, for no particular reason except that we had German neighbors and a German teacher. My grades in math and science were quite good, unlike those in history and English. But I applied myself, always completing homework on time and trying hard.

Though starting freshman football in 1966, I quickly gave it up after facing a brutal tackle by the oversized Henderson brothers. I blacked out, broke my elbow, and wound up in surgery. I concluded this was not my sport and subsequently switched to cross country running and tennis. I was gifted at neither, but was on teams that won numerous regional championships. I was a part of something, and it was fun.

By chance, in June 1967, President Lyndon Johnson traveled to Glassboro to meet with Soviet Premier Alexei Kosygin. The two leaders had agreed to meet in Glassboro because the town was geographically halfway between the White House and the United Nations headquarters in New York. It was a compromise. My father was on the town council at the time and actually welcomed Johnson to Glassboro. Though he tried to get me into the welcoming event with him, the Secret Service said I appeared too young to attend. Still, it was my first close-up of some Cold War drama, and it fed a small kernel of interest.

My parents demanded that I attend church with them every Sunday, complete with the requirement to wear a suit and tie. Some of my friends did as well, but it was not a welcome activity. Still, I was recruited into the church choir; and by the time I graduated high school, we had made a quasi-rock album of religious music and were traveling around the East Coast giving concerts in churches. Perhaps it made my growing love of rock music respectable. My ho-hum rock band was always looking for any jobs to be had, finding few, but practice we did. The songs of the late 1960s—underscored by the shocking deaths of Janis

Joplin, Jim Morrison, and Jimi Hendrix—seemed to paint a new way of being, a break from the postwar generation of civility. In 1969 several of us almost hit the road for Woodstock. One member of the band did, but never got past the New York State Thruway.

During my younger years I was a member of the Boy Scouts, rising to the rank of Life Scout. I enjoyed the camping trips and discipline, and made a hobby of collecting merit badges. I frequently felt that I had to constantly strive to achieve more to prove myself. But, by the age of 17, I was convinced I knew all I would ever need to know about life, and I felt very confident in myself.

College, of course, changes everything. My confidence collapsed when Harvard, Princeton, and Yale rejected me. My grand-father had bequeathed me some money to attend a New England school. He had graduated Yale, and I felt that I had let him down. I wound up attending Tufts University in Medford, Massachusetts. I am not sure why. I had never heard of it. Still, it seemed like a nice, quiet school. I moved away from home for the first and last time.

My first year at Tufts was challenging. I had no friends and felt totally isolated. I quickly discovered that I had never learned to write cogently in high school, that I knew next to nothing about history, and that my Latin was structured but hardly functional (or relevant). My first English professor came in on day one ranting to the wide-eyed freshmen that the lyrics to the Simon and Garfunkel song "Sound of Silence" made no sense and that the song was gibberish. Actually, it was he who made no sense. No one challenged him. No one believed him. No one liked him. Everyone was insulted by the slur on what felt like our generation. And the song took on special meaning.

But we had to learn to have opinions to defend. I scraped by.

The next few years I increasingly focused on political science and foreign languages. By my sophomore year I was working on Russian and German. French soon followed. During two of the summer breaks, I traveled to Germany and worked as a bartender. It helped a lot. The languages seemed easy enough, and the political science was needed if I was going to law school someday, wasn't it?

By my senior year I took a course on constitutional law and received a very poor grade. The books seemed so thick and the material so dry that I grew dizzy. At the same time, I received the results of my LSAT exam, which was necessary for admittance to a good law school. They were not good. That night I put all the law school applications in the trash and decided to study international relations. I had no aspiration to become a diplomat, which seemed too distant, but rather I would join a company somewhere, or work as a translator.

After Tufts, I attended the Johns Hopkins School of Advanced International Studies in Bologna, Italy, and then in Washington, D.C. The program of study at Johns Hopkins introduced me to international economics, but my focus for the two years was the Cold War conflict of ideologies, and the failed revolts of Eastern Europeans against Soviet domination in the postwar period. The topics played nicely into the Cold War, which I was increasingly intrigued by.

After graduation, I worked for a small French company in Washington for a year, before being offered a summer internship with the Berlin city government. I immediately packed my backpack and sold my car. My girlfriend had just left me, Elvis had died, and the job had little potential, so it seemed like a good time to go. I headed to Berlin with no intent of returning to the United States for ten or more years. I did not inform my parents of my departure until I called them last minute from a pay phone at Kennedy airport.

The Berlin internship was designed to indoctrinate young people from the three western Allied countries defending the city: U.S., U.K., and France. I was there with one other U.S. intern, and one U.K. intern. It was great fun. The city was divided; east-west tension was high. The wall was the focal point of everything. After two months the internship expired. I wanted to stay in Berlin, so I enrolled as a non-degree student at the Free University. My German had progressed to the point that I easily won admittance. I began attending seminars about Berlin's status and Eastern Europe. My studies entailed some reading, no real tests, and not much in the way of papers. In fact, there were not even any grades. I qualified to live in a student dorm for about $35 a month, and eat at the student cafeterias for $2 a day. It was a comfortable existence, and I was meeting growing numbers of Germans.

During the ensuing months, I traveled around Germany calling on academic institutions in the field of international affairs to chat about their activities. I knew I would eventually need a job, and I needed to make contacts. In March 1978, I called at *Haus Rissen*, an international institute in Hamburg, to discuss their seminars and research. By chance, after chatting with me, they offered me a position on their international staff. Apparently, very few German-speaking Americans called on them out of the blue, and they thought they could use me in their program.

In late 1978, I took the written exam for the U.S.

Foreign Service at the consulate in Hamburg. As a graduate student in international relations, a number of my classmates and I took the test every year, wherever we were. And every year we all failed, even with our master's degrees. However, around this time I had somehow managed to pass the written exam. I paid little attention since I was quite content living as, what I considered at the time to be, an "academic drifter."

By the end of 1979 my contract in Hamburg ran out, so I moved to the Paris Atlantic Institute for International Affairs. I did not have a job there, but I had some meager savings remaining. I just took my suitcase and moved. I found an inexpensive studio apartment and parked myself in the library of the Atlantic Institute for several months. I wrote articles on international affairs, published several of them, and prepared applications to return to graduate school for a doctorate. By mid-1980 the Atlantic Institute had no money or jobs to offer, so I moved to the University of Pittsburgh and immersed myself in a PhD program in political science. I found the work stimulating but not overly demanding, and imagined myself teaching political science within a few years. It seemed like an easy path.

Suddenly, in December 1980, I received a letter from the State Department inviting me to join the Foreign Service the very next month, in January 1981. It caught me completely by surprise. I was not expecting to join the Foreign Service. None of my peers had. In a matter of days I was headed to Washington.

CHAPTER TWO

KEY BRIDGE

JANUARY 1981

It was a sunny January day as I stood at the window of my hotel room at the Key Bridge Marriott Hotel in Washington. I was gazing across the Potomac River at the Washington Monument pondering its magnificence and wondering what the world held in store. It was an inspiring vista; one that I was now beginning to relate to in an entirely new way. It was the first week of January 1981, and I had just arrived in Washington after accepting an invitation to join the Foreign Service of the Department of State.

I had nary a clue of what to expect. The decision to surrender to the Foreign Service had been laced with reluctance. I had spent a number of years living and working in Germany, and traveling around Europe, probing the contours of the Cold War. Most recently I had been lecturing on international relations at the International Institute for Politics and Economics, *Haus Rissen*, in Hamburg. It had been a good job dedicated to East-West affairs. I was called on to lecture several hours a week in German to mostly German audiences. Being a U.S. citizen, I was looked upon as the "representative" of U.S. views. I spoke about U.S. foreign policy, the Cold War, and European integration. I was actually earning money for what I learned in school, and that had real appeal. I faced a constant barrage of thoughtful critiques from my listeners, and learned more about the world and my own country than I ever imagined. Germans love to posit profound questions about the meaning of things, and I was red meat for any concerns, as Washington was viewed as Germany's Big Brother. I was publishing a stream of articles on a wide variety of international themes. I had saved some money and vacationed around Africa each year. It was adventurous and I felt like I had arrived where I wanted to be.

THE AUTHOR ATOP THE BERLIN ZITADELLE IN LATE 1977

In 1980 I enrolled in a PhD program at the University of Pittsburgh and planned to work on East German foreign policy, a defined but growing topic at the time. By late 1980 I had lined up substantial funding for dissertation work, a solid record of academic achievement, and I was planning my next research sojourn to Europe. The Foreign Service intervened. Around early December I received a letter from the State Department inviting me to join a new class of officers starting in early January 1981. It put me off balance, as my plans went in a different direction. Still, I did the due diligence and consulted with a variety of my professors. "What should I do?" I implored of them. One after the other, each of them decidedly recommended joining the State Department over becoming an academic. They noted that academic salaries were stagnant and unimpressive, and jobs were scarce. They said that at least I should not starve at the State Department. I was reluctant, given my visions of funded dissertation work in Europe, where my network of contacts resided.

I phoned the State Department to inquire further. They said they were offering me a position as an economics officer (one of four "cones," or designations for new officers, the others being political, consular, and administrative). I told them that even though I had published and worked a bit on economics, I was more interested in political work. They immediately said that was fine, and that they would be willing to enroll me as a political officer. I took the offer.

Gazing out at the Washington Monument in the brilliant afternoon sunshine, I began to ponder what diplomacy might be all about. Despite being rather introverted, I was quite self-assured in those days, and felt as if I understood all the problems of international affairs already. I wondered what more the State Department actually knew. My years of lecturing and relative youth had provided an exaggerated sense of self-importance. But more than that, I had reveled for years in the independence and freedom of having no financial, familial, or other commitments. I told myself that if I started to become overly "institutionalized" in the State Department bureaucracy, I could always just leave. No problem. Just leave.

I then thought about the ongoing Iranian hostage crisis. U.S. television had been broadcasting each night the number of days U.S. diplomats had been held hostage inside the U.S. Embassy in Tehran. This crisis generated true American patriotism, and I was no exception. It seemed that President Jimmy Carter had consistently been unable to make any progress on this issue despite sporadic efforts. Now we were getting a new president, who would be inaugurated shortly. He was casting a long shadow even before the inauguration, speaking in tough terms about Iran and the Soviet Union. Indeed, it seemed that after Ronald Reagan's November 1980 election win, State Department Deputy Warren Christopher was finally making some incremental progress in back-channel contacts with Iran. It seemed to me at the time that the projection of toughness (in demeanor, at least) was critical to effective diplomacy. This was surely a lesson of the Carter years.

I had followed the Carter presidency closely from my perch in Europe, and never forget his quick dispatch of his own Secretary of State, Cyrus Vance, to Moscow in March 1977, some two months after Carter's inauguration. Vance had prepared all sorts of cooperative proposals designed to propel U.S.-Soviet relations into a new era. He arrived in Moscow and immediately banged his head on the chilly mistrust that were hallmarks of Leonid Brezhnev and Andrei Gromyko (known widely as "Mr. No"). He returned home empty handed after projecting a myopic go-get-'em approach devoid of any calculation of strategic politics or Soviet interests. It reflected a certain American belief that "if we can just sit down and talk openly, we will get along." Indeed, this rather folksy, innately American notion of sitting down and being understood sounded fine, but it rarely worked when confronted with hard alien political calculations. I had spoken with many Soviets in Germany and even Moscow and found them devoid of flexibility and "understanding." Talking was import-ant, but negotiated change could only be achieved in inches.

As the sun reflected over Washington, I wondered how an administration such as Carter's seemed to have performed so poorly. Carter had been renowned for his long hours working and analyzing issues. He was engaged and engaging. He was viewed as intellectual and smart. His national security advisor, Zbigniew Brzezinski, was a fabled academic. Gee, I had even spent weeks studying his mammoth opus, *The Soviet Bloc*, in college. It was a key textbook that always kept by my side. He was an intellectual giant for me, the person with all the answers to the Cold War. How was it, then, that we had made so little progress with Moscow and Brezhnev? How was it that the Soviets started deploying SS-20 missiles targeting Western Europe at exactly the time that the contemplative Carter and the intellectual Brzezinski came to the White House? How was it that even the Europeans, especially the Germans, were demonstrating against U.S. "belligerence" when the Soviets were actually deploying missiles? Then I remembered the Camp David Accords, perhaps the one major success of the Carter years. What went right there?

During this reflective moment, I reminded myself that the world was larger than Europe. Indeed, I had planned to pen my dissertation on East German foreign policy in Sub-Saharan Africa. I had published on this issue already in London. One could fight the Cold War anywhere. It was the great game for diplomats. Even in the far reaches of Angola, Ethiopia, and Mozambique, the East-West conflict was playing out in both ideological and military terms. Perhaps the Foreign Service would cast me in that direction.

The sun was starting to set over the U.S. capital on that early January day. Nations had interests, and interests in power. I had always believed in power, not necessarily just military power, but the actual use or projection of strength. Diplomats did not carry guns. To project strength and get results, I felt then that diplomacy required solid acting and clever ambiguity. Reagan was an actor. Maybe he would usher in a gold age of diplomacy.

The next day I started training at the Foreign Service Institute in Arlington, Virginia. It was like starting high school. Everyone seemed to have unfathomable backgrounds and complexes about what they were doing. Explanations of rules and regulations quickly ensued, including passing out copies of legislation in the smallest of fonts. Suggestions for reading articles about foreign affairs and diplomacy were pressed upon us almost daily. And then there was the deluge of speakers, one after the other, day after day, on what diplomats do: practicing languages, writing cables, making protests (demarches), filling out travel vouchers, obtaining passports and visas, and puzzling over the structure of the State Department, writing evaluation reports, classifying documents, and conducting consular work. Then came the instruction on how to eat in formal settings. Demonstrations of placement of forks and spoons were soon followed by questions about how to consume goat eyes when in the presence of some king, without using your left hand. I began to have doubts about service in the Middle East. Then came security talks about avoiding being overrun by bands of thugs in your apartment in Kinshasa. Africa started to seem iffy.

Next came the Myers Briggs test of personality types. The State Department seemed to think there was always great wisdom to be found in these explorations of psychological preferences. Virtually all of the new diplomats came up as introverts, and the few that were not were visible a mile away. This fun was followed by an off-site experience where we gamed a negotiation over nuclear missiles (after some grand escalation, I wound up nuking the other side; the opposite of expectations what a real diplomat should do). We then reviewed the "lessons" of the Iran hostage drama. It was emphasized that when we were abroad we would need to keep in close touch with political oppositions and not listen only to host governments. After Iran, that seemed pretty obvious to us in the classroom; but only until you got into the field where it suddenly became dangerous. Finally, we all donned blindfolds and wandered around in a room to experience "different cultures," whatever that meant. Such an exercise was probably designed to be a bonding experience, though I found that, in the subsequent years, no real bonds had been formed among my classmates.

The incoming Foreign Service class that January consisted of 52 new officers, the same number of diplomats being held hostage in Iran. It was pure coincidence, but it struck me as odd. My class-mates were from all walks of life: one mid-career dentist, one retired school teacher, the widow of U.S. Ambassador Spike Dubs (who had been executed in Afghanistan in 1979), several young university graduates, several older academic drifters, and a good sprinkling of those who had no link or relation to international relations whatsoever. It was a most diverse and unbonded group.

After two months of training, we were provided the list of jobs we were being assigned to. We were told that we would be sent to locations we knew nothing about. The explanation was that this was part of the department's "globalism" policy of developing general-ists who knew a little bit about a lot of things, rather than specialists who knew a lot about only a few things. It was emphasized to us at the time that Henry Kissinger had blessed this approach to diplo-mats. I guess that made it right. I eagerly welcomed whatever they wanted to pitch at me in those days. I was relatively young, eager, and certainly already spending my paycheck of $19,000 a year in my head, even if I went to Kinshasa. But most of my career I never got past thinking that intentionally trying to produce a diplomatic corps of globalists, could possibly result in a corps of dilettantes. Indeed, later experience taught me that when Congressional, White House, and Cabinet officials visited embassies, it was exactly the experts who knew those countries best that were sought out first. Country knowledge and language fluency were the keys to being an effective diplomat overseas, even if Washington discouraged expertise. Of course the reality and policy rarely converged.

So I flagrantly ignored the admonishments about trying to work in areas of past experience. I headed downtown for a chat with the German Desk in the main State Department building in Foggy Bottom. I wanted them to know I was around. I started off where I had left off. I was not a rebel, but I knew what I wanted to do. I was immersed mentally in the Cold War, and Germany was the front line.

CHAPTER THREE

WEST BERLIN: PEACE MOVEMENT

(1981)

I am anti-American. Go home. Get out of here!" the young German screeched as he leaped up onto the stage and shook his fist in the air. He was no older than 17, but he had the sympathies of the crowd of several hundred peers cheering him on. I tried to project a sense of sullen sadness as I endeavored to inject the audience with a sense of angst about deployment of hundreds of Soviet SS-20 missiles, which were pointed at Germany. I noted that annihilation was only a matter of seven minutes away, and that the United States was in Berlin to guarantee Berlin's freedom and security. He was unreceptive, and his teenage friends were emboldened more by his bravado than his logic. The "panel discussion," at one of Berlin's larger high schools, grew tense. The moderator tried to regain control, noting that the U.S. diplomat was simply trying to describe the larger picture. The U.S. position hardly prevailed that day, even though, or perhaps because, this was 1981 Berlin.

The German peace movement of the early 1980s was loud and rowdy. It erupted amidst a sea of angst perpetrated by the Soviet intermediate range nuclear SS-20 deployments and the worsening climate of the Cold War. Berlin attracted activists, more than anywhere else, because the city was not a legal, integral part of West Germany. In fact, the West German compulsory military draft law did not apply to residents of the city. Many young Germans enrolled in the Berlin universities, or took up *pro forma* residence in the city, just to avoid the military draft. This nourished a very vibrant youth underground that coincided with substantial sympathies at the time for all demonstrations, as well as for the RAF (Rote Armee Fraktion) terrorist group, which was at its zenith. Demonstrations involving upward of ten thousand marchers were almost weekly occurrences in the city, usually simply clamoring for peace while shutting down the main traffic arteries througout downtown West Berlin. Ronald Reagan's early signals of interest in the "Star Wars" defense systems instilled in the German youth scene with a sense of purpose.

VIEW OF BERLIN WALL SEGMENT FROM U.S. ARMY HELICOPTER FLYING OVER WESTERN SECTORS IN JULY 1981. PHOTO BY AUTHOR.

Adding to the colorful diversity of the city, the United States, United Kingdom, and France maintained substantial garrisons with some twelve thousand troops inside the city limits. Those troops drove their tanks around Berlin's forests for training, and soldiers with M-16s were regularly riding public transportation along with civilian commuters. There was a distinct sense that Berlin was an outpost on the central front of the Cold War; and that it was a city occupied by military forces, just waiting to be overrun at any time. All the while, Berlin served as an incubator for pacifist activism and anti-establishment youth.

After joining the Foreign Service in January 1981 and completing two months of introductory diplomatic training, I was delighted to receive my first diplomatic posting at the center of east-west German conflict. While most of my colleagues were dispatched to countries they knew nothing about (the idea being to create "generalists"), or assigned to visa jobs (processing long lines of applicants in "visa mills"), I somehow evaded this fate by introducing myself to the German Desk on my own time and initiative, and inquiring about Germany. Within days, my self-introduction to the secretary of the Country Director Tom Niles led to my behind-the-scenes recruitment to the political section in West Berlin.

My first supervisor, Political Section Chief John C. Kornblum, sat me down on arrival and asked what I thought I should be doing as a first-tour diplomat in Berlin. I thought that was very cool. I told him I knew several politicians and students from my previous years in the city. I suggested that I could ring them up for drinks and chats. We agreed that I would seek to decipher what young and radical Germans were up to, what made them tick, and whether they truly hated America. I felt like I was in my element.

Berlin was abuzz with debates about peace and war. I quickly became a frequent and sought-after speaker at panel discussions about security policy and peace. My very rare ability to speak publicly and in detail about security policy in fluent German (true language fluency was commonly undermined in a service that was devoted to globalism and superficial expertise) was an entry card to many heated debates, as the young Germans wrestled with their devotion to pacifism amidst the fear and threat of the Cold War. Each of the youth organizations of Berlin's political parties actively cultivated discussions about security policy. This provided unlimited access to people who in later years populated the German political landscape.

While courting debates and young activists over beer, in dark Berlin watering holes in the evenings, I spent days wrestling with reports for Washington on what young Germans cared about, and why U.S. deployments of new intermediate range Pershing II nuclear missiles did not reassure them. I tried to decipher why the Germans were more prone to offer concessions for progress in inner-German relations and with Moscow. Talks were often delicate. There were lots of chats about German identity and soul. Though there was little effect on policy, my readership in Washington began to grow, principally because I was deciphering real views by real people who were very critical of my country.

The former chairman of the Federal Reserve, Arthur Burns, was U.S. Ambassador to Germany during these times. David Anderson was the minister in Berlin, the senior diplomat in the western part of the city. Burns would occasionally visit Berlin. His ponderous demeanor complemented the gentlemanly nature of his ways. I arranged a few meetings for him with various representatives of the peace and youth organizations in Berlin. He was one of those rare people who actually came to listen, and was not interested in lecturing people as to what to do; rather, he wanted to learn. While leaning back, cradling his precious pipe in good banker style, he absorbed substantial criticism of U.S. policy, while quietly responding—almost in whispers—on the importance of talking to his German guests. For a junior officer as myself, he was a towering giant and role model, though he had little of substance to contribute to the debate on security policy. He did not win over the young people but they did respect him, and he managed to put a contemplative and human face on Cold War diplomacy.

THE AUTHOR IN 1981

I was enjoying my first months. Among others, I invited a former German professor to lunch and paid what I considered an enormous amount for wine and food. Ekkehart Krippendorf had come of age from the 1968 rebellion in Germany. He had always seemed to me to be close to a certified Marxist and quasi-eccentric. In fact, Krippendorf would have his students (of which I was one, several years prior) attend general strikes in Bologna, Italy, rather than attend class. He claimed that the demonstrations were more relevant. The dialectics he taught were intellectually vigorous, and unique. He was also influential within the German peace rebellion of the early

1980s. I often wondered how it was that such an enigma could reconcile savoring fine wine in a Berlin restaurant with a representative of the U.S. government. Krippendorf and I never managed to cross that divide, but he did provide additional color to my reports on the thinking of peace activists.

Cold War Berlin was complex. Few understood the ins and outs of the city's legal status. In addition to working the youth scene, I was also designated the "U.S. secretary" to the Allied Kommandatura. "What the heck was that?" I wondered! The Kommandatura was the meeting place of the western Allies, who held the supreme Allied legal sovereignty in and authority over the city. Sounded awesome. But to me, it was a dank, dark, eerie building in the Kaiserswertherstrasse that was brimming with mystery and buried history. It surely had ghosts roaming its low-light reaches. You could almost hear yourself breathe, walking its long hallways. Indeed, one of the heavy prewar chandeliers in a hallway narrowly missed killing a staffer when it suddenly took an unprovoked plunge from the heights. Ghosts, no doubt.

Nevertheless, each month, the U.S., British, and French commandants in Berlin would pull up in front of this unimposing yet enigmatic building, march up the broad stairway inside, one by one symbolically deploy each of their ornate hats in their designated places on a small table in the foyer, and then sashay into the large first-floor conference room. As a newcomer to diplomacy, I was totally agog at the pomp and ceremony, even though its practiced nuance never changed. The commandants assumed their designated places on different sides of the magnificent wooden conference table. They perched behind small national flags designating where they were to sit. They then worked through rather anemic agendas of issues theoretically "affecting" the security or status of Berlin. I was one of the half-dozen in the U.S. delegation. I enjoyed the meetings, at least until the French spoke. They always insisted on speaking in French, and I was less than fluent. But I tried to nod knowingly that I understood. Because the meetings were more symbolic than substantive, there was rarely substantive policy to address.

The Kommandatura was an arcane place. Nothing had been done to maintain the building since the war. The Soviets had participated in the meetings with the three western commandants until 1948, when the Soviets abruptly walked out during the first of many disputes that shaped the Cold War. They never returned. Despite the subsequent multi-decade boycott of the Kommandatura by Moscow, the three western commandants worked through the decades with the invitation open to the Soviets to return at any time. Indeed, the picture of the last Soviet commandant hung on the wall (at least through 1982) behind that side of the conference table where the Soviets were assigned to sit. Their table flag always was placed on the table at the monthly meetings, and their chairs at the table remained vacant—waiting.

I often wondered what would happen if they just walked back in. Moreover, there also were large offices in the building kept vacant for decades awaiting the return of the Soviets. In one of those offices resided a refrigerator-sized safe, locked shut since 1948. It is not clear what was inside, and I was always speculating with my staff about what dark secrets from Stalin might indeed be hidden there. We never opened it. Somehow, the legal theology (i.e., a mixture of policy, beliefs and diplomatic ambiguity) of the city was premised on maintaining a seat at the table for the

Soviets to resume a presiding role in Berlin at any time. This state of affairs was deemed critical to maintaining the aura of Allied (not German) sovereignty over the city, and this status was at the heart of the 1972 Quadripartite Agreement on Berlin, which was responsible for alleviating Cold War tensions in and around the city. With clever twist of phrase the Agreement permitted the four powers to have differing legal understandings of Berlin, but with enough flexibility to manage differences in practice. Hence, the policy was to defend the status quo of Berlin, and someday the Cold War would end.

The Allied Kommandatura was the supreme legal authority in occupied Berlin. As such, it had the authority to issue orders, referred to as BK/Os (Berlin Kommandatura Orders) and other edicts with the force of military law. However, by 1981–1982 it was a subdued operation. The western allies created committees to deal with public safety, law, budget, and other ad hoc issues. However, most business related to airspace safety through the air corridors and at Berlin's airports, *de jure* "supervision" of the Berlin police, "liaison" to the city government, and monitoring issues relating to the "status" of the city. The commandants endeavored to ensure that no east-west provocations took place, that the city officials avoided the issues of "safety and security" (which were reserved for the allies), and that military operations in the city were controlled and coordinated.

For example, at one time we had a Polish aircraft hijacked to Tempelhof airport in West Berlin. Given U.S. responsibility for the airport and police, we became an integral part of ensuring that police action was appropriate (to our needs) and that the plane was returned to Poland. In some ways, occupied Berlin was like running your own little country. Allied forces, which were intertwined with the respective Allied diplomatic services, were more influential than most diplomats in other corners of the world.

The Bonn government funded for the most part the tripartite military occupation of Berlin. The Kommandatura provided an annual budget to the Bonn Government, which in turn provided funds through the Kommandatura for the three allies to conduct the "occupation." This was essential to maintaining the legal fiction that Berlin was not an integral part of West Germany, but still retained "ties" to West Germany, as established in the Quadripartite Agreement of 1972. The three military organizations in Berlin were heavily subsidized, and military and diplomatic life in the city was generous. This made diplomatic work all the more enjoyable.

My first government house in Berlin had some 11 rooms, multiple bathrooms, a heated garage, and lawns with caretakers. I was overwhelmed to see this and receive a paycheck as well. All my belongings fit inside one trunk and several suitcases. I wound up using only two or three rooms of the entire house. It came with porcelain service for innumerable guests. The U.S. Mission in Berlin had a commandant's guest house on the Wannsee, as well as a yacht club (now housing the American Academy in Berlin) with various boats on the Wannsee. I took one of my radical youth friends sailing one day, thinking how much fun a diplomatic career was turning out to be. It was not cocktails every day at a beach bar, but it was occasionally close. The U.S. commandant's boat (also called the "ambassador's boat" when he was in town) had a full-time captain. We used it regularly for catered tripartite Allied lunches with our French and British counterparts, cruising the Wannsee while eyeballing the East German border guards patrolling the waterways for refugees. But amidst the luxury, political unrest was real.

THE AUTHOR IN AXEL SPRINGER HOUSE AT THE WALL 1982

On September 9, 1981, the current secretary of state, Alexander Haig, visited Berlin. He was the first high-level official to visit since the 1980 election of Ronald Reagan as president. Haig's sojourn took place at the height of youth demonstrations and the youth housing/squatter movement in Berlin. When Haig got to Berlin he held a speech at the Chamber of Commerce and visited the town hall in Schöneberg, where Kennedy had delivered his "Ich bin ein Berliner" speech. It was a dramatic day, in which parts of the city had to be closed down due to the large and often violent demonstrations against Haig. I was driving around with one of our security officers, Steve Raburn, who was so concerned about his personal security that day that he kept his chrome-polished Colt six-shooter on the seat next to him.

Indeed, when we arrived at Rathaus Schöneberg—where Kennedy had met welcoming crowds—a sea of belligerent demonstrators with an extremely agitated anti-American bent surrounded the town hall. The demonstrations had been organized by the youth wings of the SPD and FDP, led by people with whom I had routinely been meeting. But the demonstrators were almost out of control. They were demanding that the United States not deploy nuclear missiles in Germany to counter the growing Soviet SS-20 missile threat to Western Europe. Raburn and I were unable to break through the demonstration to reach Haig at the town hall. The police, some with blood streaming down their faces, warned us to turn around as the town hall was totally closed off by the mob. We did not have to abide, as we were technically in charge of the Berlin police. But things were getting bad. The police had to call in water cannons to clear a path for Haig. It seemed like a war zone to me.

On June 11, 1982, President Ronald Reagan made his first visit to Berlin. It was a very tense event. At the time, the German leftists despised Reagan as a warmonger. When he arrived in the city, the police confined the peace movement to conducting large demonstrations in the downtown area of the city. Cars there were set on fire. Numerous arrests were made. Reagan came to the Charlottenburg Palace, in a leafy and sedate Berlin suburb. He spoke to a crowd of some 5,000 invitation-only guests who were carefully screened in advance of the event for friendliness. The entire event was tightly closed off, but well publicized. Reagan reportedly wore a bulletproof vest for the speech. The Secret Service took aim at my ribs nicely when I inadvertently wandered too closely to the president, a lesson to be remembered. Before and during the visit, I was meeting with some of the people who had been organizing the demonstrations against Reagan.

I was able to provide some colorful details to Washington about those demonstrations in advance. Indeed, after the events, a German college friend of mine visited my home to complain bitterly over drinks that I was personally responsible for having had him arrested for demonstrating against Reagan. There was no truth to the allegation, but it betrayed the belief among young Berliners that the Allies ran the Berlin police. In fact, we had the authority to do most anything.

During the early 1980s Berlin's youth scene also entailed young people moving into old and abandoned buildings, setting up as squatters. It was the thing to do. Many were protesting rents or lack of housing, but most were simply anti-establishment. It was fashionable to protest. A good number of these young people fueled the weekly peace demonstrations, and led occasional rampages around the city with Molotov cocktails. Tossing paving stones at the police was fairly common on the fringe of every demonstration.

One time I recruited a German friend, Martina Nitke, to take me on a visit to some of her friends, who were among Berlin's squatters. The squatters were quasi-anarchists with a distinct disdain for government and the western allies. We entered a dark, musty building not far from Checkpoint Charlie. It seemed the electricity was out. Young Germans in grunge attire roamed the hallways aimlessly among candlelit rooms. Martina did most of the talking in order to minimize the risk of my being identified as member of the western forces in the city. We chatted about nothing in particular beyond living conditions and musings about police takeovers. We never considered the danger, but somehow there was a sense that "discovery" of a diplomat among the sometimes-violent anarchists could be misunderstood. We wandered around the building chatting with several of the inhabitants. It was risky but exciting for a junior diplomat.

Of course, Allied diplomats were able to enter East Berlin via Checkpoint Charlie, without visas or any other restrictions. Visits to the east were exciting. I would occasionally visit my counterparts in the U.S. Embassy to the GDR in East Berlin. Their relations with the government of Erich Honecker were not good, and they had little to do of interest. They also did not enjoy the bourgeois housing and lavish lifestyle we had in West Berlin, thanks to the Allied Kommandatura budget paid by the Germans. At one point, I drove to a Soviet military base in East Berlin and walked into the equivalent of the Soviet military PX shopping store to see what they were selling. Perhaps I wanted to see if I had the nerve to do this—walk into a Red Army facility on my own. It was a most dismal commercial experience. I recall toothbrushes and toilet paper, but little more. The atmosphere was charged with suspicion but no one challenged me. It stood in stark contrast to visits by the Soviet military to the American PX in West Berlin's Zehlendorf. The Soviets rarely entered our facilities, but they liked to patrol the parking lot in their Jeeps. Sometimes it seemed just like the movies. Indeed, one day while I was eating lunch in the Zehlendorf PX cafeteria several alleged movie producers approached me, asking if I might be willing to participate as a backup actor in a Hollywood spy movie. I think the Foreign Service had some regulation against that. The road not taken.

Perhaps a truest enigma was the monthly luncheon ceremony at Spandau Prison, where Hitler deputy Rudolf Hess resided as the lone prisoner. The Soviets were still participants in this four-power Allied effort. Each month, custody of the prison (and prisoner) would rotate between the French, British, Soviet, and American forces. The monthly "turnover ceremony" entailed a formal ceremonial event followed by a festive luncheon for two or more dozen officials. There was never any discussion about the "prisoner" and certainly no mention of him by name. Such discussion was prohibited by custom for reasons that were never clear to me. But Rudolf Hess was alive in those days. Just a whisper of sighting of him walking the grounds was grounds for admonishment. The meal, which I always enjoyed, was a highlight of Berlin's special place in history. It was another cornerstone of Berlin's status that we desperately tried to protect during the Cold War. After Hess's death, in 1987, the prison was dismantled and a supermarket built in its place. But the towering walls of Spandau Prison remain etched in my mind forever.

It was during this period that the East German Secret Police (Stasi) began to keep a file on me for some reason. I confirmed all of this when I obtained a copy of that file decades later, in 2009. The East Germans diligently followed me about and documented every time I crossed into East Berlin or East Germany. Curiously, their reports noted that I always obeyed the speed limits. When I went into a bookstore on several occasions to look at books, they interrogated the shopkeepers after I left and obtained details of everything I said and every book I purchased. They also asserted, incorrectly, across the entire file spanning a decade, that I was employed by the Central Intelligence Agency. Some observers argued that the Stasi routinely did this to ensure that they retained bureaucratic control of the files for certain individuals. Still, I found the other details of what they recorded to be fairly accurate.

By late 1982 I was assigned to move on to another posting. Washington personnel told me I could choose to stamp visas in Guyana or Bangladesh, and that I was going to be globalized in new regions. I declined to respond to those suggestions or answer phone calls. I was not even sure where Guyana was. Instead, I introduced myself to the Soviet Desk. Tom Simons was country director for the USSR. He worked closely with the German Desk, as they constituted the two critical fronts in the Cold War. He visited Berlin during my time there, so I took him for a road tour of the city I knew so well. I knew the best places to peer over the Wall, and the best restaurants with "subversive" atmosphere. I desperately hoped that Simons did not notice when I wound up driving down a one-way street the wrong way. He never said a word. It worked. I was soon assigned to the U.S. Army Russian Institute, in Garmisch-Partenkirchen, for a refresher course in Russian before heading to Moscow. Curiously, the Russian Institute seemed staffed largely with dissidents and exiles from the USSR. It was useful, but more so for skiing.

While dozing over Russian verbs in the picturesque Bavarian Alps, I chanced to stop for gas one day just as a gorgeous young Bavarian blonde stopped to do the same. Utilizing all of my quick-witted diplomatic faculties I watched her drive off without a word uttered. However, her unique car adorned with Mickey Mouse figures ensured that I might spot her again. Indeed, two weeks later I spotted her speaking with a friend. I stopped my car and immediately invited her to coffee. She turned me down icily. I did not give up. After stumbling across her at her workplace, I maintained the pursuit. After a month she agreed to drinks and a rather hectic affair. With my departure for cold war Moscow looming, the options

GARMISCH
WEDDING 1983

became marriage or separation. I pressed hard to convince her to fly off into the unknown far away. She came around. After a bucolic marriage in Garmisch in early 1983, we bounced off to a one-room cockroach infested hovel in the heart of communism. Speaking no Russian and only broken English, she recalls it as a very trying time.

CHAPTER FOUR

MOSCOW: HUMAN RIGHTS

(1983)

The ground rumbled with what sounded like hooves pounding ever closer with increasing speed and intensity. I rapidly looked to my left and then right to see what was creating the unnerving quakes. But my mind could not wrap itself around whatever reality was engulfing me. I was caught at the center of the Cold War. It was July 4, 1984.

Over a dozen panting, excited and neck-less, muscle-laden heavyweights in plain clothes rushed out of the bushes straight at us. The other diplomat, Jon Purnell, and the middle-aged Soviet woman, Lina Tumanova, were as shocked as I. There was no chance to comprehend what was happening. With four attackers overcoming each one of us, we were instantly immobilized. One attacker hung heavily on each arm, yanking and twisting them behind our backs with gleeful outbursts of force that were apparently too long restrained. I managed to grab my Soviet-issued diplomatic ID card from my shirt pocket and screamed "diplomat" as the scuffle ensued. The man intent on unhinging my elbow grabbed the document with a slight glance and stuffed it back in my pocket to be ignored. My arms were twisted even more tightly behind my back as the attackers started dragging the three of us away. With three to four husky wrestlers dragging each of us, we were soon packed into several unmarked vans and driven off without so much as a word.

One of my captors was so excited by his own efforts that he bit his own lip, producing a stream of blood flowing down his face. But he was unfazed. What was happening? Was this an official action? Were these terrorists, or some splinter group? Where were we being taken? We had not a clue. Our entreaties went unanswered. The event was pure emotion.

After a few minutes on the road, with my arms pinned behind me, I noticed a Soviet militia vehicle join in front of our van. I breathed a sigh of relief at this indication that I might be ensnared in some kind of official action. Shortly thereafter, the vans turned off into a side street. Purnell and I were bundled with prejudice into a two-story building and forcefully deposited into two chairs across from a desk, in a long, Spartan room. Half a dozen captors stood around the door, making clear that any attempt to resist or run would not succeed. There was no explanation, despite my repeated appeals to diplomatic status.

After some time, a middle-aged man entered the room and seated himself behind the desk facing us. He said nothing. Another man entered and offered us each a cup of tea, which Purnell and I vigorously refused, using the occasion to invoke the diplomatic immunity of the Vienna Convention on Diplomatic Relations in our very best Russian. Steaming tea cups were nonetheless placed in front of us, left to simmer away untouched as tempers edged up.

The man across the table then whipped out a foldable ID case, flashing some small document before our eyes, and introducing himself as a colonel in the Soviet Secret Police (KGB). He wanted to officially identify himself, he explained, before declaring that we were both under arrest for anti-Soviet agitation and propaganda and would be imprisoned. He explained that we had "violated" our diplomatic status, which was now null and void, and that we would be tried and sent to prison. He ignored our incessant appeals to diplomatic protocol. He questioned us about the Soviet woman we had been meeting, and about the various documents we had collected from her at that time. We did not respond.

After half an hour a man entered the room, set up a small table, and carefully arranged a number of documents on the table in front of us. He then perched on a stool in one corner of the room and began to snap dozens of photos of us with the documents on display. The makings of a Stalinesque show trial began to take shape.

After a long hour of fidgety waiting, a short, pudgy man entered the room and seated himself quietly in a far corner. The KGB colonel announced to us that this man was from the Protocol Section of the Soviet Foreign Ministry. On cue, the ministry man announced that our diplomatic status was violated and we were criminals who would now be sent to prison. Despite our protestations as to the legality of the arrest, the Soviets stuck to their script over and over. I began to think that my tour in Moscow was now over and I would be deported shortly. It was shocking, but it was Cold War Moscow, and several of my colleagues in the embassy had already been ejected.

After almost two hours, the U.S. Deputy Consul General

Marsha Barnes (my boss) unexpectedly marched into the room. A strident lady exuding magnificent confidence and ire, she waltzed in, announced to all present that she was there to confirm the identities of Purnell and myself. Believing she had then checked some magical legal box, she then instructed Purnell and me to stand up and walk out with her. The consul turned to depart when the KGB colonel suddenly blew a whistle. Chaos ensued. Dozens of pounding feet from the neighboring room converged on the rebellious Barnes and forcefully threw her back into our room and into a chair. It was then announced that she too was under arrest. Her protestations as well fell to naught.

After another thirty minutes of squirming uncomfortably, Barnes was told that she could leave. However, she was advised that Purnell and I remained under arrest for anti-Soviet agitation and propaganda and would be going to prison for a long time. She walked out and departed the scene. I was beginning to worry that a minor faceoff was now erupting into an international event. Another long half-hour crept by with no words. Suddenly the phone on the desk rang. The KGB colonel answered with a grunt. After listening a bit, he hung up. He announced that we could leave. Purnell and I stood up and walked out, never having touched the tea, but with adrenaline coursing.

On our arrival at the embassy, we briefed Ambassador Arthur Hartman and senior staff, before turning to the task of drafting a detailed, highly classified report for Washington. It took most of the day. Everyone was convinced that Purnell and I would be declared *persona non grata* by the Soviet government within hours. We were told to begin making plans for being quickly thrown out (usually with 24 hours' notice) of the country.

Because these events transpired on Independence Day 1984, Purnell and I were expected at the embassy's official July 4 reception that afternoon. Unsure what our future was, we attended, wondering how much more time we had left in Moscow. At the reception, we sighted the pudgy apparatchik from the Soviet Foreign Ministry Protocol Section who had declared our status invalid earlier in the day. We did not speak with him and he ensured an early getaway for himself.

By the time the reception ended, news organizations across the United States were reporting excitedly on our arrests earlier in the day, noting the growing tension in the U.S.-Soviet relationship. President Reagan issued a statement on the incident, and we learned that Washington was preparing to eject several Washington-based Soviet diplomats in the event that Purnell and I should be expelled. It never happened. We don't know why. Despite blustery statements and posturing on both sides of the Atlantic, Moscow took no further action against us.

The Soviet dissident with whom Purnell and I had met was Lina Tumanova. She was held under Soviet arrest for over a year. We had been meeting with her to obtain documents about dissidents in the U.S.S.R. She was a relatively new contact, and one could never be sure whom to trust. Anyone could be set up in Moscow. We never learned whether she was charged or convicted of any crime, but we considered it entirely possible that she had been coerced into cooperation with the KGB. However, after a year or two of her reportedly being in prison, we were informed that she had been set free on "humanitarian" grounds. It seemed she had cancer. Several weeks later, we learned that she was found dead in her

Moscow apartment. We never learned more. Human rights work in Moscow during the Cold War generally left more unanswered questions than answered, but this was one of the most baffling incidents of the Cold War. Soviet Premier Andropov had died just six months prior to this incident. The new Soviet leader, Chernenko, was feeble on a good day. Purnell and I often envisioned a bureaucratic tug of war between the KGB and Gromyko over what to do with the diplomats caught *in flagrante*. It surely seemed the Soviets wound up confused over what to do.

Human Rights

All U.S. embassies have at least one designated "human rights officer." His job is to establish contacts with the human rights activists in the country of assignment, and prepare reports for Washington on the state of respect for human rights and rule of law in that country. Very few governments welcome foreign diplomats' snooping around to sniff out secrets of their violations. During the Cold War, the human rights officers were often targeted for intimidation and harassment. But the real pain was felt by the courageous Soviet citizens, who dared to meet with us just to have their stories told.

From 1983 to 1985 the Cold War was particularly intense. Tensions over the SS-20 missile threat to Western Europe, the shooting down of Korean airliner KAL 007 in 1983, and the exile of physicist Andrei Sakharov fueled a near total breakdown of official Washington-Moscow contacts. Many embassy officers had little to do beyond analyzing local newspapers, given the refusal of most Soviet officials to speak to them. Meetings at the Foreign Ministry often had to be requested six months in advance. When the meetings took place, the Soviets said nothing of interest. But the human rights officers were always working, meeting in dark corners around the country with courageous souls, day and night.

I can't say that I wanted to work on human rights. Ambassador Hartman decided to ask me to work in this area, even though I had a day job in the consular section my first year. I was very upset by the assignment. I knew that by dealing with the enemies of the Soviet state, the Soviet government representatives would not deal with me again. This could undermine my diplomatic future and would most certainly undermine my dreams of playing a larger role, down the road, in Cold War politics. I had a severe fit of anxiety over taking on the role, but in the end I submitted to the Service, and began to sneak around the streets of Moscow in the late night, meeting the champions of freedom in the U.S.S.R. After several months, I took over the portfolio of human rights on a full-time basis and never looked back. Indeed, as things turned out, I became the only person in the embassy who had the opportunity to speak quietly with real Soviets, who spoke honestly and openly.

One most confiding dissident had the courage actually to visit me in my apartment block, despite it being watched at a perimeter by Soviet guards. Olga Korzinina was a dissident of about twenty years of age and had solid connections in the Samizdat (underground press) movement. I would pick her up in my car at a set location on a street corner, drive her past the Soviet guard, into my housing complex (largely occupied by Angolan and a few U.S. diplomats, but also infested with rats and cockroaches), escort her inside to my apartment, put a film cassette into the video player, and begin acting like we were watching a film (a popular activity in closed Soviet society). The entire time, we would handwrite notes

back and forth to one another about what was going on in the dissident movement. We never spoke, but my Russian improved quickly. After several such meetings, she subsequently informed me that
she was often arrested after our meetings, and usually held for several days of questioning about what she was doing in the apartment.
She considered it harassment, and appears to have never been held
more than two weeks. She took it in stride. I was amazed that she
could endure this. She harbored a deep hatred of the U.S.S.R.

Refusenik Trial

Other dissidents were less fortunate. Jon Purnell and I made
an attempt to monitor the trial of Alexander Yakir, a Russian refusenik (person refused an exit permit to emigrate to Israel) who
had been picked up for draft evasion, even though he was too old
to serve. Yakir's parents were close friends of the embassy and we
visited them frequently and openly; but the son had never been a
political activist. The arrest of their son, for no apparent reason,
caught the parents and me by surprise.

On the day of the trial, Purnell and I entered the courtroom
and tried discreetly to take seats in the back. The proceedings
opened with an aura reminiscent of a Stalinist show trial. No jury.
Just accusations. The three judges and "defense attorney" spent
their time flinging questions directly at the hapless defendant, sitting alone on a small, almost-stage to mumble his own hapless re-
plies. A Soviet citizen wishing to emigrate like Yakir was certainly
suspect. His views were an insult to and slander of the Soviet state.
It was more an assortment of bombarding accusations than "prov-
ing" anything. It was sad, and the outcome was certain.

YEVGENNIY & RIMMA YAKIR IN MOSCOW CIRCA 1984

After some two hours of such proceedings, the chief judge declared a break, and noted that the courtroom was being changed to one down the hall. He adjourned the session with suddenness. What was this about? All observers, including Purnell and I, filed out of the courtroom and started down the hallway toward the new courtroom. However, at the doorway, Soviet militia were posted. As we ambled to the threshold, they grabbed us and told us to wait with them outside. We waited. All other observers were allowed into the new courtroom. The doors were then closed and locked by key. The militia stood guard and declined to respond to our questions why were not permitted inside. They said not a word. About an hour later, Yakir was convicted and sentenced to the maximum two years in labor camp. We never saw him again. Sometimes it seemed hard to grasp that such things were actually taking place. But I often thought back about the descriptions of Stalin's trials, and imagined little difference with what I was seeing. I was dazed by the reality of human rights struggles, and awed by the courage of those heading to the camps.

On another day, we attempted to attend a trial of another friend. We never even made it to the courtroom. As we tried to enter the building we were immediately arrested by Soviet militia and placed in a militia van. Also in the van was a CNN reporter with a camera quietly rolling. We all had a heady ride to the militia station before receiving a warning and being released. But the CNN footage found much use on U.S. television every time Purnell and I faced the Soviet militia.

Pentecostals Rush the Embassy

We met with various religious groups, including Pentecostals from the Soviet Far East. They were deeply religious but provincial in outlook, with little understanding of international politics. Their plight was most difficult to comprehend given their extreme geographic isolation and their profound religious beliefs. At one point, the Pentecostals were so frustrated by religious persecution, a group of them traveled to Moscow, stormed past the Soviet guards outside the embassy, and rushed inside the first doorway into the embassy. They surprised everyone. However, they were then trapped by a second, inside door controlled by embassy Marines. They could not get into the embassy, but they were protected from the Soviet militia peering through the outside door at them. It appeared that the Pentecostals, some of whom I already knew, were trying to get into the embassy in order to set up a protest vigil against the Soviets, request political asylum, and force an international confrontation. Ambassador Hartman summoned me to discuss what to do. I was then dispatched to meet and negotiate with the Pentecostals, and find a way to get them out of the embassy. No one really cared how, but this kind of incident was capable of undermining the U.S.-Soviet relationship severely.

I was able to confirm that the Pentecostals wanted to make a splash for their cause by encroaching the embassy. They claimed to me that they could not now retreat and walk out the front door without being arrested and imprisoned. The Soviet militia was rapidly summoning reinforcements in front of the embassy as the crisis grew. I suggested that I drive the Pentecostals off the embassy grounds in a car and then deposit them in some other location, away from the Soviet militia. I told them it was not possible for them to remain in the embassy. After some back and forth, they grudgingly agreed.

We brought up an embassy car and I climbed in, with the Pentecostals filling the rest of the car. I counted to three. I hit the gas and stormed out the embassy driveway through the cordon of Soviet militia and headlong onto Moscow's main ring road. Within seconds, I had a half a dozen Soviet militia cars racing madly just inches behind me. I drove as fast as possible, or reasonable, and the Pentecostals were frozen with fear. After some ten minutes of high-speed racing through Moscow, I headed straight for a major subway station and told my passengers to prepare to run as fast as possible for the subway as soon as I stopped.

I hit the brakes—and then all hell broke loose. They flung open the car doors and started to sprint away. They were far too slow. A gray swarm of Soviet militia was on them instantly, and they were forcibly dragged off for several weeks of unpleasantness. Most of them I never heard from again. I was despondent. What else could I have done? The militia ignored me; they had their prey. And human rights had suffered another defeat. I often wonder what became of these religious souls.

Bonner

Yelena Bonner was the wife of Nobel laureate, physicist, and dissident Andrei Sakharov. She and her husband were the top world-renowned dissidents in the U.S.S.R. Jon Purnell and I would attempt to meet with her whenever she was in or near Moscow, to ascertain the situation of various dissidents, including her husband, who was living in forced exile in the city of Gorky. The KGB always tried to intimidate her and her interlocutors (us). On one occasion, Purnell and I picked her up in our car from a Moscow street. We tried to be discreet but she seemed to always consider the KGB a minor inconvenience. She sat quietly in the parked car and recounted to us, at length, new developments among the dissidents and the state of her husband. During this meeting, some dozen KGB personnel suddenly surrounded the car. Each had a camera in hand and all began snapping photos from a distance of about ten feet, continuously, for the duration of our meeting with Bonner. It is very hard to imagine in real life, but it was real. It was difficult not to be distracted by their actions. It was scary and unnatural in every way. But cameras clicked on and on and on. The car was a diplomatic vehicle, so the militia would dare to challenge us to exit the vehicle. At some point Bonner would have to leave. After about an hour Bonner quietly and courageously opened the car door on her own and got out to walk away. The KGB never touched her that day. I marveled at her courage.

Odessa Is Waiting

My wife and I decided to visit Odessa, a town we had never seen but one that is renowned for its refusenik population. We had the names of addresses of several prominent people we wanted to visit. However, Odessa was known for its particularly brutal KGB intimidation. They did not let us down during our visit.

On arrival at our hotel, my wife and I went into the local Intourist Office, the state-run travel office, to ask about city tours to get oriented. As soon as we entered, several employees looked up from their desks with sly grins saying, "Welcome to Odessa, Mr. Glass! We've been reading about you in the Moscow newspapers. Who do you plan to visit here in Odessa?" My lame mumbling about being interested only in tourism elicited a salvo of chuckles. The Moscow press had been denouncing me repeatedly for several months as an agent of U.S. "special services." Nevertheless, my wife and I were provided a car and driver to chauffeur us around town; the driver appeared in every way to be part-time militia. We dutifully did the tours and sidestepped his barrage of intimate questioning.

Later, after ditching the driver, we took off around town on foot, hoping to drop in cold on a refusenik or two. However, as soon as we exited the hotel, we knew we had people behind us. We were not trained in surveillance. My job was not covert. But you could feel it, and our followers seemed little concerned with concealing the surveillance. We walked for miles to see if we could shake them, but to no avail. At any given point, we had between two and four people some thirty yards behind us. After a period of time, they would be picked up by a van, and then different people would emerge behind us. The van kept switching out the people. Sometimes they would be placed in front of us so they could pass by us, face to face. Other times they stayed behind. They frequently changed coats and even wigs at one point. Was this real? It certainly seemed unreal. We had never experienced such overt and comical surveillance in other Soviet cities. It was almost theatrical, but it did the trick; it prevented us from breaking free to call on a single refusenik in Odessa. Our human rights reporting on Odessa remained extremely skeletal.

At one point, my wife and I walked along the beach in Odessa and began ascending the majestic Potemkin Stairs from the beach back into town. As we walked up the steps, a young woman in a 1950s-style, tight brown skirt and jacket was descending the stairs right at us. Despite passing but two feet from us, her glassy eyes remained studiously fixed past us in a distant frozen stare as she clutched a plastic purse tightly under her arm. As we came close to passing, a small trap door about a half-inch wide opened in the purse, exposing a small lens, and as she passed within a foot of us she shot a series of photos of my wife and me without ever making eye contact. I was speechless. We continued to climb the staircase. A young man in jogging clothes carrying a gym bag then came down the stairs. He too, passed close, looking beyond us into the distance the entire time. His gym bag had an opening with a lens looking out for another series of photos. During my years in Soviet affairs, we had never heard of such tactics against embassy officers. We decided at that point to abandon visiting Odessa refuseniks. We returned to our seedy hotel room to watch the dozens of cockroaches climb the curtains in the room all night long.

Orlov

Diplomats operate openly but discreetly, with no training in deception. Still, their efforts can put nationals at risk. My wife and I would routinely visit with Irina Orlova, the wife of exiled dissident Yuri Orlov who held court every Monday evening in her south Moscow apartment. She would invite various dissidents, always including my wife and I. These visits were welcome opportunities to delve deeper into dissident connections that reached around the country. To discuss sensitive matters, Orlova would frequently lead me to the bathroom, turn on the bathtub water, and whisper the sensitive developments about her husband and his plight in a Siberian labor camp. Walking the dark wooded areas for a mile to get to Orlova's Moscow apartment was unsettling amidst dark shadows and the occasional

L TO R: IRINA ORLOVA, KARIN GLASS, THE AUTHOR IN MOSCOW 1985

lurking militiaman. In Moscow, it was hard for me to discern when one was under observation.

Many jolly times were had with Orlova's dissidents, frequently downing cups of illegal samogan (virtually pure home-brew alcohol). However, there was always a subliminal chill about the risks everyone was taking. These were pure dissidents who hated the regime. But they enjoyed drinking and socializing and attempting to ignore what was outside the door. In the end, one of the finest human beings of the dissident group, Sergey, hung himself at the age of 26 out of frustration with the hopelessness of the system. He was someone who was not trying to leave the U.S.S.R. or actively subvert it; he was just trying to live a young man's life with some degree of freedom and joy. He always appeared happy and gregarious. He surprised me totally by taking his own life.

L TO R: VOLODYA, THE AUTHOR, LARISA BOGORAZ, SERGEY IN MOSCOW 1985

Bogoraz

Larisa Bogoraz was another fabled dissident who had suffered more than most. Her first husband, Yuli Daniel, was sentenced to five years hard labor in 1965 in the famed Sinyavsky-Daniel trial, which marked the onslaught of dissent in the U.S.S.R. In 1968 Bogoraz led a small open demonstration in Red Square against the Moscow invasion of Czechoslovakia. She was subsequently sentenced to four years in Siberian exile. Bogoraz wrote an underground book detailing the horrors of Stalin. Her second husband, Anatoly Marchenko, was arrested multiple times for human rights work and spent many years in labor camp and Siberian exile. I visited Bogoraz occasionally in her modest Moscow apartment teeming with books. She was a frail, modest woman with sharp eyes and a raspy voice. She was extremely cautious and discreet, and I

ANATOLIY MARCHENKO & LARISA BOGORAZ IN UNDATED PHOTO

tried to sneak to her apartment as quietly as possible. She knew the KGB always had her on their radar. She was another true example of someone who sacrificed her life for freedom of expression. She was unforgettable.

The Synagogue

Every Saturday evening, for two years, I spent strolling the street in front of Moscow's main synagogue. Refuseniks from all over the country knew that U.S. diplomats would be there to chat with them and find out what was new with their efforts to leave for Israel or the United States. The results of those chats would find their way into the annual U.S. Human Rights Report or CSCE Implementation reports. However, the KGB also mastered the game, and dispatched people to work the synagogue gatherings. The KGB tried to infiltrate and intimidate. They would occasionally be out there with cameras, snapping photos of us at a distance of ten feet as we spoke with people. They would occasionally push and jostle us, depending on how robustly we pushed back. They occasionally posed as refuseniks, seeking to gain our confidence.

One particularly striking couple, Nora and Vlad, started showing up on Saturdays. No one seemed to know where they came from, but they always had nice clothes and warm boots. They seemed to us to reek of KGB. I tried to avoid them, but they were constantly asking us for favors, all of which were prohibited by the State Department. Usually it began with requests to mail letters to the West for them through the diplomatic pouch. It might then develop into requests for things from the West that were prohibited in the U.S.S.R. These items might include religious books. In one case, a U.S. diplomat tried to help bring a heart valve into the

U.S.S.R. However, such transactions were risky, and if exposed by Soviet authorities, could lead to expulsion by Moscow and discipline by the State Department. But it was sometimes hard to ignore the innocent wails of what appeared to be suffering individuals. Even when the temperatures were at minus thirty degrees, the U.S. diplomats were still there plodding the pavement every week. I was never so cold in my life. No other diplomats except the Canadians and Americans would show up. Human rights work was, for the most part, viewed by most other countries as an impediment to regular diplomacy between states. I credit Canada significantly for their work with us.

THE AUTHOR INTERPRETS FOR GEORGE H.W. BUSH IN COURTYARD OF U.S. EMBASSY MOSCOW IN JANUARY 1984. AMBASSADOR ARTHUR HARTMAN IS IN BLACK HAT.

Diplomatic life is always varied and unpredictable. In February 1984, Vice President George H. W. Bush visited Moscow to attend the funeral of Soviet leader Yuri Andropov. During the visit Bush also took time to address the embassy staff, including the several hundred Russians working for the embassy at the time. With no warning, Ambassador Hartman shoved me next to Vice President Bush and asked that I interpret his remarks on the spot into Russian for the staff. Such surprises always spiced up diplomatic work. I have no idea what I said, but Bush was always gracious.

Moscow bore a wealth of excitement and hardship during Soviet times. At one point, the embassy determined that the Soviets were using "spy dust" to track our movements around the country. In particular, they revealed that I was one of their prime targets. This florescent dust was surreptitiously poured into our cars and other places we might step or touch. It was invisible to the naked eye, but it left a trail from our shoes and clothes that could be followed by Soviet officials tracking us. The State Department medical division spent quite some time studying the dust to determine whether it was a health threat. The studies were reportedly inconclusive. Though I tried to be as discreet as possible when arranging meetings with contacts, none of us were ever sure we were not being watched. Arrest could come at any moment. Curiously, some U.S. congressmen loved being followed by the KGB when I would take them to meet activists.

In early 1985, U.S. Marine Corps Guard Clayton Lonetree invited my wife and me to a luncheon with several of his Marine colleagues at the embassy. It was part of a Marine outreach effort to get to know the individual diplomatic officers in the embassy. My wife and I attended and the luncheon was unspectacular but cordial and friendly. Lonetree seemed like a typical young man, with no particular insights into Moscow. Several months later, however, he was suddenly arrested by U.S. officials and charged with spying for the KGB. It was quite surprising to learn this about someone known to us. It appeard Lonetree had a KGB girlfriend whom he supplied with sensitive information about the embassy. This scandal led to an investigation and findings that the Moscow Marines were holding raucous parties with Soviet women, a definite step over all red lines. Several Marines were implicated in wrongdoing and the commission of serious security violations. One of the most distinguished U.S. ambassadors of the century, Arthur Hartman, was later forced to resign as a result of the affair, about which he claimed to have had no knowledge. It was a time when leaders stepped down for transgressions, regardless of their own lack of culpability or knowledge. It also said something about the State Department that I would see play out numerous times later: You may be discredited and even destroyed for things about which you knew nothing. Bureaucratic and political scalp hunting was real.

Coal Mine

The embassy diplomats took every opportunity to travel inside the Soviet Union in order to experience firsthand what was happening around the country. The Soviets restricted travel severely and all trips had to be approved by the Soviet Foreign Ministry several days in advance. Nevertheless, we utilized many opportunities. Most of the more senior diplomats traveled to sunny Georgia, one of the favorites due to the renowned wine and legacy of Joseph Stalin. More junior officers, like myself, were left traveling to dreary, less-pleasant places others did not wish to visit.

One such trip was Donetsk in winter. This sterile coal-mining town in Ukraine had few features above ground to commend a visit. I don't recall any tourist attractions. But my wife, Karin, and I decided to explore anyway despite the total absence of any known human rights activists in this part of the U.S.S.R. Perhaps because it was not a front in the human rights war, the local officials were unusually friendly and offered us a private tour of a

AUTHOR & KARIN GLASS VISIT COAL MINE IN DONETSK, UKRAINE

coal mine. We naively accepted. At the outset, we were instructed to shed all of our clothes, including underwear, and provided complete suits in heavy cloth due to the coal dust. The suits reeked of lye, the common substitute for soap in the Soviet Union. We were given helmets, with lamps, gloves, face masks, and oversized boots, to punctuate the experience before it even began. (Ordinary Soviet citizens did not visit coal mines.)

We were then led to a rickety elevator that appeared to be secured by little more than rope and a few boards, and quickly lowered down. It was nerve-racking. The ride down the mineshaft continued for some time. When we hit bottom, we were told we were at 4,000 feet below sea level. We were shown an emergency evacuation room to be used in case of cave-ins. I began to sweat profusely. We were led along long, low corridors with very little lighting. We were then encouraged to crawl on our bellies through a small opening about two feet high from the floor. It was a moment of high anxiety as we could only wonder if we would survive the next cave-in. Perhaps we were being led into some new Soviet chapter of harassment. We were both turning black from the coal dust as we crawled forward, nervously peering around for salvation. We entered a small underground chamber where the ceiling was about four feet high and the floor was a pile of crushed rock. Several men were working a mine face with heavy air hammers, chipping away at the face. They were totally black with coal, and several were shirtless and mask-less.

The poignant image was one of oversized, muscular Stakhanovite socialist workers. They stopped the ear-splitting machinery upon seeing us, and began chattering away with us in Russian, and answering questions about their work. They put in a plug for the wonders of socialism. They were delighted to have visitors—visitors who were fearful and wishing to get back to the surface as soon as possible. They deftly laced their answers with praise for Lenin, as I silently contemplated the prospects for a cave in. It was scary and surreal.

After our hastily scrambling back out of the confined space, the guide explained various procedures to deal with cave-ins, continuing to assure us we were safe. We returned to the surface and were treated to showers with lots of lye soap to try to remove the coal dust. It was impossible to scrub off. We subsequently were invited by the director of the mine to a lengthy luncheon with flowing amounts of vodka. It was a wonderful experience to have had, but rather unique in the Foreign Service. My subsequent report to Washington about visiting a coal mine drew an unusually large number of readers.

Siberia

Another working trip my spouse and I undertook was to Irkutsk, Siberia, in late December. It was as desolate a place as I have ever witnessed. The temperatures were around minus 35 degrees celsius. There was little to see except for an overwhelming nothingness. The town was more of a village-like collection of old wooden huts with fences around them. The hotel was as sparse as anywhere we visited. The floor of the hotel room was so cold and dirty that whenever I got up to go to the bathroom, I donned my heavy boots to walk around. Meals were things to forget. They usually consisted of generous menus with many offerings, none of which, however, were available when we were dining. If there was any meat at all, it was some kind of processed chicken. With luck, one might get some cold peas from a jar. Knowing to be prepared, we always traveled with our own supply of ramen noodle soups and chocolate bars for in-room consumption.

In Irkutsk, my wife and I walked up the main street in blinding snow to a house that was reportedly occupied by the only American citizen in Siberia. No one in the embassy had ever met him. He was renowned far and wide for flying the American flag in front of his hut in the middle of Siberia. When we arrived at his entrance, there was no flag flying. We tentatively knocked on the door. An elderly Russian woman answered. She seemed to be a housekeeper. She said the man was away. She did not say where. She invited us in. She sat shivering in her rocking chair with a blanket wrapped tight. No tea, just small talk. There was a small wood stove in the room, but the temperature was still well below freezing. We had a polite chat about nothing and then departed. Impressions of Siberia in winter. We never found the American.

Central Asia

I embarked on another trip with my supervisor, Geoff Chapman, who wanted a taste of adventure that always seemed to be coming my way but eluding him. We decided to go to Dushanbe in Central Asia. As soon as we got off the plane and headed for town, the local police arrested us. Chapman was ecstatic. He was finally in action. The police explained that they knew who we were. They wanted to know what we were planning to do in their town, so they could discourage us. We explained that we were just looking around as tourists. They were profoundly skeptical. They said they would be watching to make sure we did nothing more than that. They detained us for an hour or two before letting us go, warning us not to meet with any citizens. They had us stopped alone in the hills outside Dushanbe. What could we do? We obeyed.

By mid-1985 it was easy to leave the hardships of Moscow. Gorbachev was now running the country, but there was little indication of the radical changes to come. Gorbachev was known in the early months for trying to battle alcoholism in the country. This was causing some consternation among my Russian friends, almost all of whom drank vodka whenever they could get it. At the same time, Gorbachev's new concepts of *glasnost* and *perestroika* ("transparency" and "transformation") were only starting to attract some press attention. After two tours overseas, my fate was to return to Washington for a few years in the State Department. My first journey into the halls of power was coming.

CHAPTER FIVE

WASHINGTON: BERLIN DESK

(1985)

The return to Washington from any overseas posting is the most difficult of transfers, both financially and professionally. Moving into a temporary apartment in Rosslyn, Virginia, and living out of a suitcase for weeks (sometimes months) until finding a permanent place to reside, was never fun. Spouses absolutely abhorred these moves. However, trying to bring about such a move while working full time (which usually meant more than ten hours a day, plus long commutes) did not facilitate amelioration of the upheaval.

Still, arriving from dreary Moscow made anywhere seem delightful. The colorful lights and shopping beyond the drabness and slate colored sky of Moscow were exhilarating. I began my first real job in "powertown" in the Office of Soviet Affairs as executive assistant, focused on ad hoc assignments from the director. It was a temporary, two-month bridge job until my assignment on the Berlin Desk opened.

The Cold War was raging and the Soviet Desk was a key

place to be. The office was working hard to arrange ministerial meetings, as well as a summit between Ronald Reagan and Mikhail Gorbachev. There was a constant quest to flesh out the "checklist" agenda of issues to discuss. This included bilateral topics such as human rights (mostly the U.S. agenda), economic cooperation (a lot of rhetoric about small-scale projects and good intent), security issues (which meant OSCE cooperation, nuclear talks, etc.), and regional issues (mostly an exchange of views on various conflicts around the world). It was the kind of agenda designed to repeat well-worn positions and not upset the proverbial apple carts. There were few expectations of change, but just the fact of talking with the Soviets was in itself a success. The real issue, though, was the continued parrying over intermediate-range nuclear forces in Europe (SS-20, cruise missiles, and Pershing II). Any use of such weapons would obliterate Germany. Low-level talks with the Soviets had been bumbling along for five years, with little promise. Any movement here would be significant.

Given my background in Soviet human rights issues, I was dispatched to Boston in December 1985 to consult with Yelena Bonner, who was briefly visiting her relatives there at the time. Sakharov was being held "hostage" in Gorky, while she was away. It was bizarre to see her outside of a Moscow setting. Such discussions always included questions about the status and health of Sakharov, a review of the political situation in the U.S.S.R., and assurances that the U.S. government would continue in every meeting with the Soviets to press against human rights abuses. Bonner was the consummate professional; always difficult to fathom, but always sporting clear ideas on her wishes. Meetings with her were always big events for Washington.

YELENA BONNER & GEORGE GLASS IN
BOSTON 1986

After two months of unfulfilling odd jobs on the Soviet Desk, I moved into my new assignment as the Berlin Desk officer in the European bureau. There were few better jobs at the time. No one in Washington had the time or background to understand the complex legal realities of Berlin. They knew enough, however, to realize that it was a potential flash point that could, more than any other, set the world on a course of conflict. The complexities of Berlin rendered it profoundly difficult for outsiders to dabble in. For this reason, the Berlin Desk officer was usually dubbed informally the "Berlin theologian" and was generally the one person who was expected to actually understand what was happening in the city. Mumbling about "four-power status" and "air corridors" and "checkpoints" always sounded high-minded and intriguing to the State Department pinstriped set. And when the mini-crises struck in Berlin, as they inevitably did, the "theologian" was always there to bamboozle with historic precedents and footnotes. Plus, the presence of U.S. troops "on the front line" added a drama that was infectious.

One of my favorite Berlin complexities was Live Oak. It was a tripartite (U.S., U.K., France) coordinating body that was co-located at NATO, in Mons, Belgium. It was a contingency body that existed to coordinate tripartite defense of Berlin, in the event of conflict. Every year we would conduct war games to exercise command and control of the body. In late January 1986, I hosted French and U.K. diplomats to that year's game in Washington, inside the Operations Center at the State Department. A scenario was played out, with each delegation tasking respective Live Oak commanders with actions, and reporting back to their nations' respective capitals. The scenarios usually included responding to reports of the East Germans or Soviets closing down the autobahn transit routes to and from Berlin, or problems in the air corridors, such as a plane crash. In no event were the games to ever get to the point of significant hostilities, since diplomatic professionals were supposed to manage their way around an outbreak. That seemed a bit petty to me.

In 1986, the scenario had the transit route to Berlin being closed and some shooting taking place. At one point, I pressed for a significant escalatory military response, usually a go-slow approach. I convinced my U.K. and French colleagues to acquiesce to this strategy, and they reported back to their capitals. That was about as far as these games ever went. I then suggested we deploy some tactical nuclear weapons to add a sense of reality, given the growing emphasis on theater weapons. Within hours, the U.K. Defense Ministry was protesting vigorously that the game was out of control. For the first time, the game was escalated to conflict. I wanted to know what would happen in terms of planning, if conflict in fact occurred. I found out: people became scared and the game was ended shortly thereafter. Our mini–war game was a great bonding experience. But it always served as a special reminder that the United Kingdom, France, and the United States had a special responsibility for and sensitivity to stability in Berlin. It was also a reminder that Berlin and Germany remained ground zero.

Libyan Terror

Three months later, on the evening of April 5, I was sitting at home when the phone rang. A bomb had gone off at the West Berlin discotheque La Belle and a number of people had been killed. I was summoned to work, where the German Desk quickly formed a task force in the State Department's Operations Center. Our office ran the task force around the clock for two weeks as we sorted through events and options. We subsequently established that the Libyan embassy in East Berlin had been party to facilitating the terrorist blast, which killed two U.S. servicemen and injured 79 other U.S. military. In total, three people died and 230 were injured. During the ensuing days, Washington policymakers were able to quietly confirm culpability and ten days later launched air strikes on Tripoli and Benghazi. Those punitive strikes came close to killing Colonel Qaddafi.

During late 1986, east-west tensions in Berlin began to increase quietly behind the scenes, due to changing tactics of then-East German leader Erich Honecker. He seemed to be engaging in a strategy to destabilize West Berlin and West Germany by facilitating the movement of large numbers of refugees from developing countries into West Berlin, where they could seek political asylum and then be relocated to western Germany. Germany had one of the most liberal asylum laws in the world, once a refugee crossed

German borders. Honecker was willing to help them. Because there were no western border controls into the western districts of Berlin, anyone could enter those districts, regardless of documentation, if they were allowed to exit the east.

The East Germans had long been cultivating special relationships with countries such as Ethiopia, Angola, and Mozambique. They began, in a large way, to permit citizens from these and other countries to fly into the East German airport at Schönefeld, where they were then transferred by bus to East Berlin proper. From there, they were directed to walk unhindered into West Berlin and request political asylum. West Berlin turned none back, and relocated most into West Germany. The flood increased significantly during late 1986 and early 1987. It was seen as a GDR strategy to destabilize the city and West Germany. It caused substantial consternation for the Bonn government, which had no way to stop the influx without taking some action that would undermine the delicate balance in Berlin and their own desire to build relations with East Germany. Moscow seemed not to care.

As this mini-drama was playing out, Honecker decided to up his hand by slowly closing down the Berlin checkpoints to Allied military traffic and personnel while allowing Berlin civilians continued access to the east. This tactic was designed also to divide the Berlin population from the western Allies, since the restrictions only applied to the Allies. Suddenly, East German border guards were stopping Allied military (which also included diplomats, who had "military" status when assigned to West Berlin) on the eastern side of Berlin checkpoints. Because the Allies did not legally recognize any East German sovereignty in East Berlin, we refused to submit to these controls. This led to standoffs inside the checkpoint with western military locked inside their cars, with their windows up, and East German guards circling the vehicles demanding passports. After an hour or two of harassment, the travelers were usually permitted to drive in. But the antics and delays by the East Germans was the goal. It created great frustration among the three western Allies, who could enter East Berlin only via Checkpoint Charlie and never be sure how long they might be delayed at the crossing. We were being squeezed out of the eastern sector despite the guarantees of free circulation for the Four Powers in all of Berlin.

If we did not use Checkpoint Charlie, we would have to drive across the Dreilinden checkpoint into East Germany, submit to East German border guards there, and then embark on a lengthy drive back into Berlin. Such a scenario for Berlin theologians was unthinkable, as it would signal *de jure* Allied "recognition" of East German sovereignty over Allied military travelers to East Berlin. Very few people understood the legal ins and outs of this issue, but it was quite real for Allied insiders. Of course, our Berlin diplomats, including myself, all marched routinely to the Soviet embassy in East Berlin and complained bitterly about these East German ploys. But the Soviets were not particularly responsive to the idea of reining in their German proxies. Though the Soviets had ultimate responsibility for security and stability in their sector of Berlin, they also had to contend with whatever conspiratorial plots Honecker was serving up privately.

By the spring of 1987, problems at the checkpoints had become a true policy headache for the United States, the United Kingdom, and France. The Germans did not seem to mind, as the East German tactics at the checkpoints did not affect German citizens.

Likewise, Allied capitals did not seem to mind all that much, as the restrictions affected only soldiers and diplomats in the field. Even the Bonn government did not seem to care, as German citizens were not affected. Only the three Western powers present in Berlin suffered. On the margins of the June 1987 NATO ministerial meeting in Reykjavik, then-Secretary of State George Shultz raised this problem in his regular "Berlin" side meeting with his French, U.K., and German counterparts. It was unusual for what seemed to be a "technical" issue in Berlin to rise to such a level, but everyone was intent on avoiding disturbances in Berlin. German Foreign Minister Genscher was pressed to the cause. More pressure was subsequently exerted on the Soviets, and the West Germans had their own discussions with the East Germans. The ministerial communiqué coyly speaks about improvements in inner German relations, which was more wishful thinking than reality. Shortly thereafter, though, the East German regime suddenly stopped all harassment at the checkpoints and the flood of asylum seekers through East Berlin tapered off. There was no significant press reporting on what seemed to me at the time to be a significant retreat by the East German regime. It was a great success for diplomacy, provided one understood it. The press missed the entire backstage drama.

During the Reykjavik ministerial meeting, I sat in my hotel room one evening, listening to the live broadcast of President Ronald Reagan's 1987 speech live at the Brandenburg Gate. I had worked hard on organizing this, his second visit to the city, but there had been a lot of back and forth on the speech over just what it should say. The stumbling block was the fact that Berlin was celebrating its 750th anniversary in 1987 and everyone wanted a softer, friendlier atmosphere in Berlin. People wanted to ignore the refugee problem and the checkpoint challenges. Berliners on both sides of the Wall wanted some harmony and cooperation, and even joint celebration to the extent possible.

Governing Mayor Eberhard Diepgen of West Berlin received an invitation to attend a theater event in East Berlin with the East Berlin mayor. This created significant Allied head-scratching and anxiety. The Allies and West Germans did not officially recognize any East German sovereignty over East Berlin, and therefore the East Berlin mayor had no authority or standing to issue any kind of official invitation or exercise any official act of this sort. However, it was becoming increasingly popular among West German and West Berlin politicians to try to build contacts to the east. Such contacts in the name of *Ostpolitik* ("new eastern policy") were applauded by West German voters, and portrayed as a German contribution to overcoming broader Cold War tensions. The East Berlin invitation to Diepgen provided him with a larger-than-life political image right at the nexus of east-west relations. At the same time, were he to recognize the East Berlin mayor by accepting the invitation, he would *de jure* undermine part of the Allied legal position on Berlin, which held the Soviets as the sovereign authority in East Berlin. We generally frowned on such "salami" tactics of "selling off" a slice of "Allied status" in exchange for some public glad-handing with East Berliners. In the end, Diepgen declined the invitation. Perhaps the clarity of Ronald Reagan's "Tear Down this Wall" statement made clear to many that East and West still differed dramatically.

Sitting in my hotel room in Reykjavik, listening to Reagan, I was stunned at this phraseology. Earlier drafts of the speech, which I had seen, were much more restrained, seeking to speak in terms of cooperation in the city in light of the 750th anniversary. Indeed, the Reagan remarks that day went in the opposite direction of the NATO ministerial communiqué paragraph on Berlin, against Diepgen's apparent predisposition on invitations, and against what I had seen in early drafts. As a diplomat, I was shocked and unsure how this fit into our efforts to celebrate Berlin's anniversary. Reagan had suddenly refocused the entire Berlin stance, reminding us all that the Cold War was still real as long as the Wall was standing. I felt like diplomatic efforts at reconciliation, even in small steps, were going to stall.

Being the Berlin Desk Officer included regular visits to the city, including the east. On one or two occasions I met with people such as Heinz Kosin, ostensibly a researcher at the East Berlin Institute for Politics and Economics (IPW). Kosin was believed at the time to possibly be working for East German intelligence. However, given the paucity of contacts we had with any East German officials at the height of the Cold War, my few contacts, such as Kosin, that predated my government service, were intriguing. I met and talked about the 750th anniversary of the city, and warned against improper salami tactics. Kosin was an engaging interlocutor and defended East Germany. We never found any common ground—but we always talked. Some 25 years later, I obtained from the Germans a copy of the file kept on me by East German intelligence (Stasi) in those days. The file had a detailed and extremely accurate and detailed, almost verbatim, report on my discussion with Kosin at the time, possibly submitted by Kosin. Also included were photos of me in East Berlin, walking into the embassy and talking with another U.S. diplomat. The file again identified me as working for the CIA.

Instead of cozying up to East Berlin for the 750th anniversary of the city, we in Washington decided instead to focus on the western part of the city by giving it a gift. For this event, we elected to present to the city an exact replica of the statue of General von Steuben standing in Lafayette Park, in front of the White House. We worked to have precise casts made of the White House statue, and had a new statue cast. It was unveiled in Berlin in 1987 and currently resides at the corner of Clayallee and Hüttenweg, in Dahlem. After German unification in 1990, the city of Potsdam also obtained a second copy of this very same statue as a symbol of new friendship with the United States.

CHAPTER SIX

DUCK POND

(1987)

It was early summer and I needed to get out of the State Department building to breathe. I walked down 21st street to the National Mall and turned left. After a bit I came to a small set of ponds at the base of 19th Street, where the ducks led their ducklings around as the sun sparkled on the ripples from the wind. It was always a peaceful place for me, one where I could also glimpse the Washington Monument and Lincoln Memorial.

I wondered about the Cold War and what would happen next. Despite the new nuclear systems in Europe, the growing fascination with Ronald Reagan's "Star Wars," nuclear doomsday scenarios, the East-West sparring in Berlin, and what seemed like growing terrorism in the Middle East, I had the sense that the world was relatively stable. It was hard to predict or anticipate change, and the status quo always seemed the most reliable predictor of what was coming.

Even though Gorbachev had been in power over two years, change seemed to be limited to atmospherics. Talk of *glasnost* and *perestroika* seemed to be just that—talk—which was fine but not earthshaking. The Warsaw Pact seemed as united and solid as ever. NATO seemed like the most professional and capable of organizations. The EU was pressing its growing unity among the West European countries. Indeed, the world I knew was quite comfortable, with just the right touch of occasional drama. Was any great unraveling coming? I did not think so. I could not then imagine how anyone could manage the Soviet Union without an iron fist. Even though we had passed through the demise of Brezhnev, Andropov, and Chernenko—a generation of geriatrics—Gorbachev promised more youth and energy. But systemic demands would compel continued repression. The strains in society and the economy were just too extreme to manage things any other way, I believed.

I perceived that day a clarity about freedom and democracy like never before. I came to truly believe that the test of any society is its protections afforded to—and, even, courtesy toward—its most outspoken dissidents. That notion seemed to have been well recognized by our nation's founding fathers, and seemed to always set the United States apart from other countries around the world. My speeches in those days often referred to Berlin as a beacon of freedom. But in some ways, this was more a reference to the United States, which underwrote postwar Berlin's freedom. For me, freedom was an absolute value that had to be pursued constantly. It could not be compromised. It was in abundance nowhere more than the United States. I felt like I had spent years trying to make this case to foreign politicians and opinion-leaders.

As Ronald Reagan's legacy grew in his second term, it became easy to sell the American way overseas. His defense secretary, Casper Weinberger, projected strength and willingness to deploy proportional force. Secretary of State George Shultz was, in my view, a ponderous, moderating influence on all. With hindsight, I found Shultz the best secretary of state I ever worked with.

I watched the ducklings trailing behind their mama around the ponds. Sometimes one or two would venture a bit out of reach, exploring farther than desired. Or were they lost? Would I follow the siblings, or wander off the trail? Chewing on my peanut butter and jelly sandwich that day, I realized that diplomacy was capturing me, and my independence was eroding. The powertown Washington tended to do that to people. At what point do you begin to sacrifice your soul to some great, imagined good?

CHAPTER SEVEN

TOKYO: BEAR BOMBERS & SUSHI
(1987)

In the summer of 1987 it was time to face a new assignment again. I was being groomed to stay in Washington, to take over my supervisor's position, overseeing Berlin, East Germany, and inner-German affairs. Though aghast at the prospect of staying two more years to suffer the life and death dangers of Washington's 495 beltway and the financial hardships, there seemed no escape. Suddenly, however, I received a phone call from the Japan Desk. Japan? They asked me to come visit with them. When I arrived, I was suddenly offered a job in Japan, as the "Soviet watcher" at the embassy. During the Cold War, most major U.S. embassies had Soviet watchers to keep an eye on Moscow's antics in key countries or regions. These were not the toughest jobs, requiring less host country expertise, but I was still fairly young and curious. Why not try something new? Maybe I should globalize a bit. I went to consult with one mentor, Mark Parris, who was now running the Soviet Desk. Should I stay or go? Looking me straight in the eye, he said that if I remained in Washington working on Germany, something I had mastered, I would be "thinking with my head" and that if I went to Japan I would be "thinking with my heart." I was off balance. I had always been overly cerebral. Still, having never been west of California, I decided to leap at the chance to do something totally different and new, albeit still sidestepping Guyana and Bangladesh. Within a month I was on my way to Tokyo and the strangest world I have ever visited.

On arrival at Narita airport, for the first time in my life I felt like a true foreigner in an impenetrable culture. I had not a word of Japanese in my linguistic repertoire, and only a few days of State Department "area training" in preparation for this adventure. I doubt I would have found my way out of the airport were it not for my new supervisor, Don Keyser, driving out to the airport to pick us up. As one of the State Department's top Asia hands, fluent in Japanese and Chinese, Keyser whisked my wife and me into the country and straight to the embassy. He guided me through the ins and outs of Japan, revealing an uncanny intellect and insight into the workings of the country.

Though I had few tools to penetrate the Japanese mindset, my job mainly entailed deciphering the "thinking" of key policymakers in the Japanese foreign ministry. Luckily almost all Japanese diplomats spoke fluent English, so my chances of survival were not completely lost. I was to focus on the Soviet Union, Europe, the Middle East, and arms-control issues. Compared to prior jobs, this was a straight-line diplomatic job: I was to set up meetings with various directors at the ministry, call on them over a steaming cup of the inevitable green tea, question them for up to one hour— but no longer—on the subject of my next report to Washington, and take no written notes (diplomatic protocol discourages such crutches), all the while memorizing verbatim what was said. On returning to the embassy, I crafted a long line of reports detailing Japan's perspective on these issues and provided my thoughts about their approaches. It was fun and productive.

Of course, everyone expects that diplomats must host lavish lunches and dinners in pursuit of their insights. The unlimited funding in Berlin had truly spoiled me. In Tokyo, though, entertaining was hardly possible, given the enormous cost of even rudimentary affairs. At the embassy, we carefully divided up all the "representation" money allotted to us by Washington each quarter of the fiscal year. This money was to be used to fund lunches with "contacts" in Japan that would help further the U.S. national interest. Given the extremely high expense of Tokyo, I was left with just about enough money for one single lunch for one single Japanese contact every three months, as long as no wine was included. Few others in the embassy fared better. The Japanese officials I hosted at these modest events seemed to understand, if not sympathize with, the rather frugal offerings of the Americans, but were always perfectly polite, chewing away on rather unappealing morsels in a cafeteria-like environment. It was embarrassing most times, especially given that such mundane lunches would cost over two hundred dollars.

The Japanese, on the other hand, had unlimited representation budgets; this was partly due to cultural differences. The Japanese foreign ministry on numerous occasions hosted me at lengthy dinners with unlimited courses and drinks, with waitresses in kimonos waving fans and ensuring that one's sake glass was never less than full. It was more exotic than even Hollywood movies. I learned that these meals cost the host government more than $500 a person. Given the expense of dining in Japan, my wife and I went out to dinner only once on our own, over the course of three years. It often seemed that Japan had won the commercial wars in those days, and was capturing the wealth of the world.

As the Soviet Union was the most significant "issue" I had to work with, I concentrated my efforts not only on the Japanese ministry, but also developed some rather tentative anemic relations with the Soviet embassy as well. Visits to Soviet embassy receptions were highly desired for their offerings of free caviar in those days. During the late 1980s the main issues for Tokyo were the contested yet uninhabited islands to the north of Japan known as the Northern Territories. The shoving match between Tokyo and Moscow had been going on for years, and was nowhere near being resolved. The Japanese felt historically obliged (there were many Japanese graves on the islands) to stand firm to their claims, and the Cold War Soviets were unlikely to show anything but resolve in their claims to the islands. Every few months, Moscow would dispatch Bear bombers to fly over the islands as a demonstration of that resolve and to liven up Japan. The Japanese would diligently go on high alert, and inform us of the approaching threat. We would send profound analyses of each "crisis" to Washington, and that would be the end of it—until the next time. It was a subtle reminder that the Cold War persisted even in Asia.

Tokyo was where I also first began to develop some knowledge of Afghanistan and the Middle East. The Japanese government was quietly permitting, as was the United States, some domestic support for the Mujahedeen (forerunner of the Taliban) efforts in Afghanistan. One renowned Japanese citizen, in particular, would travel regularly to Afghanistan and participate in Mujahedeen operations, sniping at Soviet soldiers from the mountains. I achieved a personal meeting with this "Japanese Mujahedeen" and conducted a long expedition into his thoughts on the battles from the Afghan mountains. He was very proud of his efforts, and the Mujahedeen welcomed him as a signal of broader Japanese support. The reports to Washington on his meeting met with applause. This was the time when anecdotes of real skirmishes against the Afghan communists were praised and later reformatted into Charlie Wilson's War.

The Japanese also enjoyed closer relations in those days with the Palestinians, especially Yasser Arafat. Given that the United States had no relations with the Palestinians in those days, and explicitly despised Arafat, Tokyo achieved a minor role. When Arafat visited Tokyo, in October 1989, I expended substantial effort in studying questions of Middle East peace before seeking views of Japanese diplomats on what Arafat was up to. Though the Japanese had no particular policy goals or messages for Arafat, the simple fact of their meetings with him was of interest in the diplomatic world. Verbose reports were conjured after my dutiful consumption of an adequate amount of Japanese green tea.

During my years in Japan, I somewhat studiously embarked on Japanese language lessons each morning before work. Under no illusion about ever living long enough to master Japanese, I managed enough spoken words for basic needs when traveling around the country or in dire need of a toilet. It was a very difficult language for me. I doubted I would get far, but I kept at it. Perhaps it was all worth it when I one day found myself at the Spring Cherry Blossom Reception with Japanese Prime Minister Takeshita standing alone and just a few yards away. Diplomatic success is sometimes reliant on opportunities seized, and I was not absent ambition. I walked over to the prime minister and in my

most polished bumbling Japanese introduced myself and congrat-
ulated him on his election. I told him how lovely the cherry
blossoms were. I remembered that there were innumerable forms
of speech for addressing exalted officials in Japan. I knew I got it wrong, but Takeshita was excep-tionally polite and fired off some comments, which sailed right by me. We shook hands over broad smiles. No report on that one, but I was able to boast about introducing myself to the Prime Minister.

THE AUTHOR WITH AMBAS-
SADOR MIKE MANSFIELD IN
TOKYO IN JUNE 1988

Former senator Mike Mansfield was ambassador to Japan until January 1989, cover-ing about half the time I was in Tokyo. He was a genuinely distinguished gentleman. He would dutifully hold weekly country team meetings with the two or more dozen senior managers of the embassy. The meetings in total were to never last more than ten minutes, and Mansfield kept to the clock with an unforgettable precision. His most famous refrain during those years was that the U.S.-Japan relationship was the most important in the world "bar none." That phrase became a standard component of our policy, however overstated it may have been. But his commitment was unshakable. During several meetings in his office with Japanese officials, Mansfield was always himself serving coffee in delicate china cups to each person in the room, despite his own trembling hands. A true gentleman loved by all.

Of course diplomats have their moments of trial. At one reception in Mansfield's home, I had mistakenly selected a glass of wine rather than the usual orange juice. Never a good idea for a serious diplomat, I clumsily brushed against a small side-table, knocking it over with a clang that resounded like a sonic boom. I was mortified as faces turned to identify the perpetrator of the disturbance. As I tried to quickly move away into the garden, I walked full gait into a closed glass sliding door. If the table had created a disturbance, the boom of my nose crushing against the glass and the annihilation of my diplomatic pride remained unforgettable with me for years. These kinds of embarrassments just were not supposed to happen in such a proper place as diplomatic Japan. I realized that understanding Japan would require a lifelong commitment.

Of course, all residents of Japan experience earthquakes. In my case, I was sitting on the tenth floor of the embassy, in a conference room with ten others, when the big one hit. The room began to sway dramatically back and forth as we pondered the sheer panic that was hitting everyone around the table. One Japanese lady grabbed others by the hand, and we all held hands wondering if these were our last moments. We waited an eternity to see if the furniture would start sliding and banging about. But after three long minutes the quake subsided and everyone began to breathe again. The quake registered 5.9 on the Richter scale. It was terrifying, but only one of a half-dozen quakes during my years there.

The largest issue during my time in Japan was the Japanese economic boom. The United States was envious and obsessed with finding a way to right a burgeoning trade imbalance. Americans were importing Sony Walkmen, video recorders, and Toyota vehicles at phenomenal rates. There was a sense in Japan that the economic behemoth was unstoppable. Trying to fathom how the Japanese built such economic success was the jealously guarded purview of the economic section alone. Others ventured views at their own peril. Yet economics touched all of us living in Tokyo. Money seemed unlimited for Japanese. My wife, who spoke limited English (but fluent German!) in those days, was paid over $40 an hour to "teach" English to ten-year-old Japanese boys. It was said that at one point an investor came to the embassy seeking to buy the entire property for cash. There was no sign of this changing by the time I departed in 1990. It was the golden age for Japan, and the Japanese, before the bubble burst.

November 1989 was huge. My daughter, Nicole, was born in Roppongi, Tokyo. Since none of the doctors or nurses spoke English, and I was equipped with three different cameras, the event was total, unforgettable chaos. Thankfully, the Japanese treated us graciously. For me the world had changed forever.

And then, on November 9, 1989, the Berlin Wall fell, to the astonishment of everyone I knew who had worked German affairs. I later learned that Ambassador Vernon Walters had seemingly alone anticipated unification, but his was a solitary view. I had spent my life on German affairs and had no idea it was coming. I had spent years lecturing on overcoming the Cold War an inch at a time, building diplomatic bridges, handshakes and smiles. I sat in Tokyo that night, holding a newborn while watching press reports and struggling to fathom what was going on. I longed to be in Berlin, just to be part of it. A scant few weeks prior, I had been speaking with a senior East German diplomat at a reception in Tokyo. The East German had told me convincingly that all was calm and well in East Berlin. It seems East Berlin fooled him too.

Several days later, U.S. deputy chief of mission J. D. Bindenagel, in East Berlin, phoned to ask if I could transfer to East Berlin immediately to assist his embassy with sorting out whatever was going on East Germany. I said I would be interested if he could get then-ambassador to Japan, Michael Armacost, to agree to the transfer. After some vigorous tussle between Tokyo and East Berlin, Washington had to decree that I would depart Japan only in mid-1990. I was to miss a good deal of the East German action (e.g., the March 1990 elections).

For a young diplomat, Japan had been a real foray into a new world. The culinary challenges were extreme: grasshoppers, live shrimp, crabs with the shell, jellyfish, fumbling chopsticks, removing shoes, bowing everywhere, grapefruits for a hundred dollars, and oceans of green tea. But it was the most pro-American society I had encountered. Japanese diplomats I knew in Tokyo would occasionally look me up in my later assignments and renew those contacts; the representatives of no other country did that, in my experience. The openness and relationships with Japanese officials was, for me, deep and lasting—something Mike Mansfield well understood. At the same time, it became clear to me that the Japanese were different from the Americans, in a multitude of ways. They were bound by cultural traditions and social expectations that formed their very being. Their politics were practiced as overtly consensual and glacial. They appeared to be the most solid of allies to the United States. But they were not us.

My supervisor from those days in Japan, Donald Keyser, was, in September 2004, charged with espionage by the FBI for spying for Taiwan. According to press reports, Keyser subsequently obtained a plea bargain, in which he pleaded guilty to possessing secret documents and lying to the FBI about his sexual relationship with a Taiwanese intelligence agent, in exchange for dropping the espionage charge. In January 2007 he was sentenced to serve one year and one day in prison, according to press reports. In the diplomatic world, it was hard to fathom such surprises that seemed to erupt from nowhere. Keyser had been one of the most talented and respected Asia hands in the State Department. He had solutions for every diplomatic challenge. He knew every issue in Asia. He had risen to our top ranks. How was it that these things happened?

My years in Japan were marked by stability. I felt that the Cold War was still out there lurking, but things were suddenly shifting. Reagan managed to get an agreement on intermediate range nuclear forces with Mikhail Gorbachev. How did that happen? How did the Soviet Union suddenly move that much? Could we take Gorbachev at his word? Hard to imagine. The departure of Ronald Reagan did not seem to threaten much change, inasmuch as he was passing the baton to his vice president, George H. W. Bush, who seemed more informed on foreign policy than anyone else in government. Reason would surely prevail. The Berlin Wall was apparently opening, but what would that mean for East Germany? Surely the East German government was not surrendering to the West. Was it some kind of new plot? The changes of that period were too swift to digest. Better to just hold on.

CHAPTER EIGHT

EAST BERLIN: GERMAN UNIFICATION

(1990)

By the time I arrived in East Berlin, in July 1990, it seemed like I had already missed most of the excitement surrounding the fall of the Berlin Wall and the collapse of the East German Honecker-Krenz government. The first free elections had been held in eastern Germany in March 1990, and a discordant array of people were elected, none of whom were known in Washington. It was a dream come true for a political officer like myself.

During the heady summer of 1990, I spent most days in the balcony of the parliamentary chamber of the Palast der Republik, a monstrous building in downtown East Berlin constructed to house their parliament and celebrate socialist achievement. It had been adorned in earlier times with huge oversized Soviet Realist paintings of the socialist superman, with ripping muscles, marching into a future of industrial achievement and equality. By mid-1990, the first democratically elected parliament, the Volkskammer, was meeting almost continuously to seek to govern events in the aftermath of the Wall coming down. East Germans were leaving the East in droves. Eastern businesses were grinding to a halt. Western carpetbaggers were fanning out, looking for ripe pickings. No one was really sure who was in charge of a political landscape now littered with all-but-unknown political parties, movements, and initiatives. I would spend hours upon hours in the parliamentary chamber listening to speakers, from a variety of new parties, pontificate on a range of issues, from defending the deeds of some of the old East German regime to appeals for immediate unification with West Germany. Speakers were often impassioned, but anything but united on any views. After the daily dose of speechifying, I would wander over to the press office of the East German government, seek out press releases of interest, listen to any press conference that might be going on, and then return to the embassy to cogitate on what it meant for my reporting to Washington. It was terribly stimulating. On the other hand, it was totally alien to the stable Cold War world to which I had become accustomed. I often wondered if we would have noticed anything if the current East German leader, Egon Krenz, had simply used the military to close the Wall back up back in November.

It was not unusual during those times to find the East German prime minister, Lothar de Maizière, carrying his own cafeteria tray while standing in line for lunch, along with all the other East German parliamentarians. He was as shy and unassuming as he was unknown. His occasional speeches to the parliament were quiet and restrained. Other notables of later German politics were Joachim Gauck, a relatively unknown pastor from Rostock with a James Garner face. Gauck would speak forcefully against the transgressions of the prior East German communists and the secret police. He was a profoundly moral voice. He later was appointed to oversee the disposition of the files of the East German secret police. In 2011 Gauck became president of Germany. Gregor Gysi, who later led the Party of Democratic Socialism, and then the Left Party, was the pied piper of all the rookie leftist parliamentarians, delivering sweet-singing twists of phrase with stinging barbs laced with Hegelian twists. Gysi was then, and remained decades later, a magnificent speaker, albeit long suspected of having collaborated with the communist regime and its secret police. At the press office, Angela Merkel was at that time the deputy press spokesperson for the fledgling government.

FUTURE GERMAN PRESIDENT JOACHIM GAUCK VISITING BERLIN HOME OF AUTHOR & KARIN GLASS JUNE 1994

Rather unassuming in those days, and certainly unknown, she later rose to become chancellor of Germany. Many other parliamentarians went on to be elected to the unified German parliament, the Bundestag.

As the summer of 1990 wore on, there were rumors that parts of the East German government around the interior minister, Peter-Michael Diestel, might be planning to utilize their control of the security services to bring about a coup against the de Maizière government, perhaps to take the country in a direction more amicable to retention of former government structures (and employees). No one really knew what would happen in 1990 Berlin. The situation was unprecedented, and there was no clear path to the future for East Germany. In August, I had a solo lunch with Diestel to try to assess the brash young man who was emerging as a strongman in the new government. Diestel was an imposing personality who always moved with a bevy of robust bodyguards. He projected an overbearing self-confidence bordering on arrogance. I could not really tell at the friendly, but ultimately non-confiding, lunch what his inclinations were.

On August 23, 1990, I remained seated in the parliament balcony watching the parliament debate unification with West Germany. It was an unusually long session, and I had been there more than 12 hours. There were many speakers for and against sidling up to West Germany. Opponents worried that they would surrender all voice over their futures and become second-class citizens inside a larger Germany. They worried that they would lose jobs, wealth, and control of their futures. Others claimed it was not feasible to remain independent with East German citizens and wealth flooding to the West.

As the evening wore on and turned to night, it was not at all clear anything particular would happen. However, a colleague and I remained listening to the debate past midnight and into the early hours of August 24. Sometime after midnight, the Soviet ambassador to East Germany appeared and claimed his (still) regular seat of honor in the balcony. Suddenly it seemed that something was happening. With very little fanfare, a motion to unify with West Germany was suddenly put to the floor. De Maizière and a few others offered brief statements on the motion. Sleepy delegates then rose one by one to deposit their votes in an urn—a procedure that took a good hour. There was no bubbling excitement per se, but rather uncertainty. The votes were tallied over the course of an hour. The president of the Volkskammer, Sabine Bergman-Pohl, came to the podium to announce that the motion had passed. That was the moment that East Germany voted to unify with the West. The parliament had just voted itself out of existence. There was applause but little more. There was an aura of bewilderment, a lack of comprehension of what had just transpired. We left the session after three in the morning, racing by foot back to the U.S. embassy to begin a stream of reporting on the changing world.

About a week or so later, the Parliament was forced to abandon the Palast der Republik; it was later condemned because it contained asbestos. It was an ironic end to one of the Communist regime's greatest treasures. The parliament decided to hold its next meeting in a bank building that later became the new German Ministry of Foreign Affairs. The meeting was held to announce and discuss the results of investigations into which parliamentarians in the current parliament had been confirmed collaborators of the East German secret police (Stasi). The session promised high drama, and it was packed with press and other observers. I could not find a seat, so the parliamentarian group of the Party of Democratic Socialism (the Communists), which was closest to the door, offered me a chair with their delegation. As a diplomat I was wary, but the seat at what promised to be a front-page drama was attractive.

The meeting started off quickly. Parliamentary officials began to identify, one by one, individual parliamentarians in the room who had been confirmed as having been covert collaborators of the Stasi in East Germany. Each was then given a chance to speak at the microphone to the crowd. I watched one member walk up to the podium with tears streaming down his face. A middle-aged male, he addressed the group choking with sobs, claiming that he had meant no harm. He said this was a tragedy and misunderstanding. He said his behavior had been perfectly normal and accepted in East Germany. He asked what this denunciation by the parliament would do to his family and children. Emotions in the room surged, but there was little sympathy. It was a melodrama right out of the days of Joseph Stalin.

Suddenly, the president of the session decided to interrupt the meeting in order to close the room to the press. I remained still in my seat with the PDS, wondering if I would be shuffled out as well. Indeed, shortly after proceedings resumed, I was also asked to leave. Bad luck. The doors were then sealed, as were the fates of numerous former Stasi collaborators, as they were denounced one by one.

Reagan Again

In late September 1990, Ronald Reagan visited Berlin for the third time. I accompanied him on this visit. We began by strolling through the Brandenburg Gate from west to east, before walking over to a large residual piece of the Berlin Wall. Reagan dutifully and with good cheer took up a chisel and pounded away at the hard concrete. He was a good actor, but seemed genuinely intrigued with the city. It was fun to be around him.

After that, we rode down the main boulevard, Unter den Linden, to the Palast der Republik, which was by then officially closed to the public. Though the building was dark and largely unused, we entered a side door in order to call on the last president of East Germany, Sabine Bergman-Pohl. It was a subdued meeting, with Bergman-Pohl managing little English. With cola drinks and coffee around a small table, we spoke about the progress toward unification, which was only two weeks away. Reagan seemed stirred but was rather quiet.

On October 2, 1990, I attended the final session of the East German parliament. This final ceremonial meeting at 5 p.m., just hours before midnight unification, convened in the old East German Council of Ministers building. A smattering of short, ceremonial speeches accompanied fancy dress, but there was no real business to transact. The session was adjourned after a half-hour, and East Germany was ended. I could barely comprehend what was happening.

After departing the parliament, I hurried back to the embassy. I found Ambassador Richard Barkley and the embassy staff in the basement holding a rather sedate party "celebrating" unification among themselves. The mood was rather somber as the future was so uncertain. We all understood that within hours the U.S. embassy to East Germany would cease to exist because its client state was going out of business.

As midnight approached, I moved on to the front lawn of the Reichstag building awaiting the big party to celebrate unification. This was where the action was. Several hundred thousand people were pouring into the square in front of the Reichstag. Fireworks were screeching and screaming in every direction. I have never seen such a boisterous celebration. I was sure that rockets whizzing by my head would hit. At the stroke of midnight, Chancellor Helmut Kohl addressed the crowd to thunderous applause and joy. This party had a profound feeling of history. An oversized new German flag was hoisted on a new flagpole in front of the Reichstag. A new Germany was at hand.

The day after German unification, I arrived at the embassy to find that the ambassador had departed post with the first flight. His country of assignment was gone. His task was complete. The entire staff was summoned to the conference room for a 10 a.m. meeting.

At that meeting, U.S. Minister Harry Gilmore, who was in charge of the U.S. mission in West Berlin marched in with his deputy, John Nix, and assumed charge. They explained that on instruction from Washington and the U.S. embassy in Bonn they were now placed in charge of what was now to be called the new U.S. Embassy Office Berlin, which included the combined staffs of East and West Berlin. They then announced a purge of the diplomatic ranks, unlike any I had ever experienced, in order to slim down the combined staff. They read a list of positions and duties assigned to the various key officers down through the ranks. The former deputy chief of mission in East Berlin, J. D. Bindenagel, was now assigned to undefined "special projects," and John Nix would take his place as second in command. The East Berlin political counselor, Jonathan Greenwald, who knew everything about East Germany, was replaced by the political counselor from West Berlin, who knew nothing about the East. Greenwald would have to seek some other job in Washington. I was made deputy of the political section. Many of the East Berlin supervisors were left without jobs and spent the following weeks seeking new jobs in Washington or elsewhere. It was traumatic and embarrassing for many who were not selected to remain. It was a human relations disaster.

The takeover was bureaucratically rather bloody and hostile, and was believed to have reflected the petty animosities and jealousies that had infected relations between the missions in Bonn, West Berlin, and East Berlin over the years. Over the following months, hundreds of German and Third Country employees of the two missions lost their jobs. Careers came tumbling down. The headquarters for the new Embassy Office Berlin was in the building of the old embassy in East Berlin. It was bureaucratically a very difficult time for all employees, the majority of whom lost their livelihoods. History was claiming its victims. The result left me more or less in charge of puzzling out the political situation in the eastern parts of the new Germany. This was a significant chore.

East Germany itself was not quite finished. The legal act of unifying did not change the real situation of most East Germans overnight. Changing a flag did not immediately change an entire political-economic system. There was widespread uncertainty about how to deal with the aftermath of the communist state. Who was to maintain order? What were the laws to be applied? How were the police to know what to do? What officials would run the towns and counties of the east? There was widespread talk of a "legal vacuum," wherein there were no laws to enforce and no one to enforce them. What was to become of the East German Army? What about the Soviet troops stationed around the country? This situation of uncertainty persisted for months, and the danger of destabilization was quite real.

I asked everyone in the political section to spend their time traveling to the towns and villages around east Germany: looking, talking, snooping, exploring, prodding, and learning. In each town they were to meet with the acting mayor, local pastor, acting police chief, or any other quasi officials they could find. They were to then report on what they were told, and what was going on in the east. In particular, they were to pay attention to law and order, and the Soviet and east German soldiers. This approach to our work lasted for several years as our team worked to present an evolving picture of developments from the local level in eastern Germany.

U.S. EMBASSY OFFICE TEAM L TO R: MIKE MOZUR, NICK DEAN, CHRYSS HERNANDEZ, PAUL HUGHES, AMBASSADOR ROBERT KIMMITT, THE AUTHOR, DEIDRE CHETHAM, BRENDT HARDT, DICK MILES, JOHN NIX IN JUNE 1992

Two weeks after unification my son, Michael, was born. It was a drizzly, foggy night in East Berlin as my wife and I sipped some champaign strolling the street just before rushing to the closest West Berlin clinic. I now had pre- and post- unification children. Would they have any idea how the world changed between their births?

Several months after unification, the Germans carved up eastern Germany and created five new state governments. These governments were populated by people elected through a rather messy, but ultimately successful, series of state and local elections. Those elections, of course, were preceded by the creation of various political party organizations. It was extremely primitive with many candidates totally unknown. I visited party conventions one after the other, for weeks on end, trying to memorize new faces and watching as western German "advisors" from the West German parties tried to educate people as to the purpose of political parties. Though the eastern German political landscape was a shifting group of unformed alliances, the western German parties came in and sponsored the creation of similar-type sister parties in the east. East Germany had actually had some political party organizations (the bloc parties) of its own, and these structures were seized on, in the early days. They evolved into new political parties to match the west German landscape with a few exceptions; Gysi's democratic socialist party stood out as the gathering point for all the former East German apparatchiks and communists. With time, this approach gained traction. When the new states were created, several western German state governments also established partnerships with the budding eastern institutions, and advised them on how to govern, manage, and lead. Many western German politicians found new political afterlives in the east, despite the lingering culture clash.

The Brandenburg state parliament first met on October 26,

1990. The parliamentarians had nary a clue what to do. I was seated with other observers. One person I happened to meet at the session introduced himself as a visitor from the western city of Düsseldorf. He explained that he was a state government employee in Düsseldorf and had been dispatched to advise the new parliamentarians on what to do. He revealed to me the script he had written for the session and who was to do what. He pointed out one gentleman hiding behind a large plant next to where the parliament president was seated. He explained that the man behind the plant was whispering to the president what he should do next. It was curious to watch the slick westerners coaching the newly emerged easterners on parliamentary democracy.

On one occasion State Department counselor Robert Zoellick visited Berlin. He had successfully led the two-plus-four negotiations, which had produced the final settlement on Germany, abolishing allied special rights and status. Basically the talks were the venue for the four victors of WWII (United States. Great Britain, Soviet Union, France) to negotiate with the two Germanies (East and West) about changing the status of Germany. It was a behind the scenes push-pull negotiation, which eventually dovetailed with the political unification. Overcoming British and French concerns with unification, not to mention Soviet issues, was no easy task. President George H.W. Bush, Condoleezza Rice, Robert Zoellick and Philip Zelikow earned great credit for orchestrating one of the most significant diplomatic successes of the century-the peaceful unification of Germany and Europe. Zoellick came from German heritage. I took him on the typical dog-and-pony show of the east. We drove to Jüterbog, a central area for Soviet troops. We had lunch with the mayor, eyeballed miles and miles of decrepit former Red Army installations, and calculated how far the east had to travel to join modern society.

During the following years I met many of the state parliamentarians, who later were elected into the united German Bundestag and achieved varying positions in the German government. Many had a hard time competing with the slick, educated, data-driven western bureaucrats. They had to learn an entirely new way of life, and how to govern. It was an evolution for decades.

From 1991 to 1993, Robert Kimmitt was ambassador to Germany. He frequently visited Berlin and was a tireless advocate for ensuring German unification and retention of the special relations between the United States and Germany. He was well respected. However, because the U.S. ambassador to Germany sat in Bonn, he was afield of the action. The real turmoil remained in and around Berlin, where 16 million former East Germans had to come to grips with a new reality.

Gulf War

On January 17, 1991, the U.S. military arrived in Kuwait for Operation Desert Storm, which was designed to drive out Saddam Hussein. Though far away, this military action had an immediate impact on Berliners. West Berlin had a long legacy of pacifism, up to unification, and East Berliners had been preprogrammed for years against U.S. military action. These trends reinforced each other. Despite the success of unification, peace demonstrations near the embassy office were immediately launched, along with vigils for peace in front of the embassy office.

On one of those days I arrived at the embassy office to find a large gathering of demonstrators on the front steps. I entered without problem. On entering, I found the Marines in full battle dress, with flak jackets and shotguns just inside the front doors. They were poised behind large columns for cover and their weapons were loaded. I asked what was happening, and was told there were big demonstrations and the embassy was under threat. I raced upstairs to Minister Harry Gilmore, who was in charge, only to find him preparing to don his own bulletproof vest. I questioned whether there was truly a threat of violence here. He was unsure. I convinced him to let me check further before we continued to escalate. I proceeded back to the front steps of the building. The crowd started protesting to me. I addressed them in German and managed to calm them down. They explained they were part of a vigil for peace, and that they feared for an apocalyptic end of the world from Desert Storm. They envisioned that the liberation of Kuwait would lead to a major escalation of conflict around the Gulf, that the oil wells would be blown up and burn for years. This would cause ecological disaster. I listened to their complaints with my best face of reassurance and sympathy, and promised to note them. I then proceeded back inside the building and reported that the crowd was mostly young teenagers with no obvious tendency to violence. The Marines stood down. The group quietly disbanded.

Several days later the demonstrations picked up again. I was standing in my office window overlooking the main street where the demonstrators were congregating. It all seemed peaceful enough. No one was belligerent, but the crowd was decidedly older. Suddenly a brick hit the window I was peering through and shattered the glass. I was stunned. Other bricks then began to fly, and within seconds other windows were broken throughout the building. I saw a number of demonstrators in the crowd suddenly pull up bandana masks to their faces as the crowd took on an ugly tone. They shook their fists at me. The suddenness was breathtaking. The German police arrived with water cannons and were soon able to disperse the group. A final memory of the peace movement in Berlin.

Inquisitors

Every few years the State Department sent around its "inspectors" to sniff out wrongdoing of any kind at its various diplomatic missions. Inspectors were frequently peer foreign service officers who were dispatched every few months to look under the bed sheets. In 1993 we were visited by "investigators" from the Inspector General's office. They interviewed a number of people in Berlin, including the author. As a rather young officer, I was somewhat terrified to be led into a room, seated in a hard chair in the middle of the room, blinded by two large spotlights pointed directly at my face, while these two "investigators" pitched questions to me from the shadows about the Berlin Document Center (BDC). Was this Hollywood, again?

The BDC was the repository of Nazi Party membership records dating from Hitler. The United States had custody of the records until 1994, when we turned it over to the German government. I wrote the evaluation reports on the performance of the director of the center. My inquisitors questioned me for over an hour about what I knew about the center, never revealing what they were looking for. I was shaken to the core. Slowly it came out that someone had complained that the deputy director of the BDC had hired his daughter for a summer job in violation of U.S.

government nepotism rules. The investigators could not figure out whether the BDC was a State Department institution (I supervised the director, at least on paper), a military entity (as it drew administrative support from the U.S. military in Berlin), or a German institution as it was, in fact, funded via the Allied Kommandatura budget. I doubt they ever figured that one out. But it reminded me of Arthur Hartman in Moscow, and the fact that, in government, the things you don't know are the things most likely to do you in. Innocence protected no one. In the end, the Berlin principal officer at the time, Douglas T. Jones, told them to back off and find something constructive to do. We never heard from them again.

Another Spy

Every few years another intelligence affair seemed to erupt unexpectedly. What better place than Berlin? On January 12, 1991, we were informed that Stephen Laufer, a South African national who became a naturalized German citizen, had been arrested by Berlin police for spying for the Soviet KGB. At the time of his arrest, Laufer had been working as an employee of the press section of the U.S. Embassy Office in Berlin. He had reportedly been working for the KGB since 1977. He ultimately spent several years in German prison before being released to South Africa.

Laufer's arrest surprised many in Washington. He was the consummate networker who was widely liked and wound up knowing many senior officials. I first met him in 1977 when I was a student at the Free University in Berlin. I attended a course on the legal status of Berlin, and found the young Laufer also attending the course. We remained acquaintances over the years. He attended my wedding to take photos in 1983. He was accompanied by Jane Boatner, the daughter of the current commander of U.S. Forces in Berlin. They had been dating for some time. He wound up working as a speechwriter for Governing Mayor of Berlin Diepgen, before moving to the press section of the U.S. embassy sometime before unification. When he worked for Diepgen, he was also working with another speechwriter, Thomas de Maizière, who later became cabinet minister in the German government. Laufer was around the power people. In August 1990, he hosted a group of friends and I at a Rolling

STEPHEN LAUFER & JANE BOATNER IN APRIL 1983

Stones concert in Berlin. He never said who paid for the tickets. His arrest was a sharp reminder that the intelligence wars were never far away, even after unification.

Toward the end of my time in Berlin, Richard Holbrooke was appointed ambassador to Germany. Controversial by nature, Holbrooke also exuded a distinct and intense intellectual curiosity about things. When he first visited Berlin, he stormed into my office in a ponderous mood. He spread out on my couch and kicked off his loafers. Rolling his eyes at the ceiling, he slowly asked what it was that I did here in Berlin. An unusual introduction it was. I explained the efforts to get to know the new eastern German politicians who were sprouting up around the new eastern states. He expressed interest in meeting some of them.

Not long thereafter, I found myself in a car with Holbrooke and his assistant, Rosemarie Pauli, on the way to Potsdam to meet

Brandenburg Minister-President Manfred Stolpe. However, there was a terrible traffic jam on the roads out of Berlin and we were at a dead stop for over an hour. Being a creature of action, Holbrooke had his assistant crank up the cell phones to various people in Washington, Egypt, and beyond. At one point he was talking on three lines to different people about global issues far beyond Germany. After an hour we gave up on the Potsdam trip, and turned around back to Berlin. Holbrooke turned to me with a big smile and said he really enjoyed the trip; he made lots of calls and got a lot done. He was genuinely pleased. There were few people who would claim to have liked Holbrooke, but I found him fascinating due to his intellect and unpredictability. Little did I know our paths would cross again.

CHAPTER NINE

HONOLULU SUN

(1994)

My mentors in the State Department were making plans to have me transferred to work on NATO affairs in Washington after my time in Berlin. It was the head and heart thing, again. It would be best for my career to return to powertown. However, the Foreign Service personnel gurus had different plans to waylay any individual ambition I might have. It was called senior training. I had just been promoted at the end of my Berlin tour, and I was informed that I was now required by a new policy to enter one year of "senior training" before embarking on any next assignment. I was permitted to choose from a list of universities, which I would attend for a year as a diplomat in residence. After years of dreary Berlin weather and a residual curiosity about Asia, I chose the East-West Center at the University of Hawaii. And off I went.

The East-West Center was relatively unstructured, with a variety of academics coming and going. It was envisioned as a meeting place for academics and policymakers in the middle of the Pacific. Amidst the bright sunshine, I spent a year reading and researching two topics of interest to me. The first was a comparison of European and Asian integration efforts, which resulted in the publication of an article. The second was a comparison of the notions of German and Korean unification, which resulted in a manuscript and several lectures. I am not sure any of these writings were particularly insightful. They seem now to have been a last grasp at order and definition in a world that was quickly losing it. Viewing European integration as some kind of magic formula that could work in Asia was little more than tool to explain why things would not work. Wishful thinking about Korean unification, after the German success, was just that. The North Korean regime had no wish to join Erich Honecker in exile in South America.

During that year I participated in numerous seminars on foreign policy subjects. I also traveled around the islands speaking about the Department of State, and rendering a number for foreign policy speeches.

The director of the East-West Center at this time was Michael Oksenberg. He was an engaging leader who believed in the coming exponential growth of China, which was his lifelong expertise and passion. Over a private lunch with me one day, Oksenberg described at length why China was destined to eclipse all other countries in Asia and would become the number-one challenge to the United States in the world. I have always remembered his words.

Hawaii was a lovely interlude. My windsurfing skills improved dramatically, my family probably spent its happiest year ever, and my growing concerns about State Department bureaucrats faded a good deal. However, it was little preparation for what was to come. After a year in the sun, I was to land back in Washington working on NATO affairs in the European Bureau, but in a Europe that was spinning out of control.

CHAPTER TEN

WASHINGTON: NATO AND BOSNIA

(1995)

The return to Washington brought with it another lengthy tenancy in temporary quarters, before moving into a new house. The financial burdens returned in exponential force as I now had a spouse and two children along. Moreover, commuting the Washington Beltway to the State Department had only become more adventurous. The new job as deputy director of political-military affairs in the NATO office left not even waking time for family matters. I began the new position on July 10, 1995. Things began moving quickly.

The new position placed me as part of a broader interagency group, which was meeting daily to review events in the Balkans. My office initially had little to do with those events, but it did provide military guidance to our NATO mission, and thereby took on an aura of the "military office" in the European bureau. However, on Friday, July 14, just days into the new job, I was sitting in an interagency meeting talking about Bosnia. National Security Council Senior Director Sandy Vershbow, a career Foreign Service Officer, chaired the meeting. Several participants began sharing unconfirmed reports that "something bad," entailing substantial military operations, seemed to be taking place in and around Srebrenica, Bosnia. Though there were no hard facts to dissect, discussion suggested that a sizable number of people were being killed. The information was too sparse at that point to act on, but there was a sense in that meeting that the Bosnia imbroglio had just exploded. Within days the Srebrenica massacre of more than 7,000 unarmed civilian men began to find its way into Western reporting. It had a distinct impact on everyone dealing with the Bosnia issue. It was a policy turning point at that very moment. There was a deepening recognition that the Bosnia conflict was spinning out of control and Washington was going to have to get involved in a big way.

Up until that point, the United States had retained an arm's-length approach to Bosnia. We preferred having the Europeans take care of challenges in their region. We were pressing burden sharing at NATO. The Europeans kept harping about their European Security and Defense Identity (absent the United States), which never really came into focus. We were content to let them wade into the Balkans. President Clinton was emphasizing, repeatedly, the importance of the domestic economy and seemed cautious on foreign affairs. During the early part of his first term, he withdrew all U.S. forces from Somalia, reflecting growing U.S. domestic discontent with the dangerous situation there. After that withdrawal, Somalia descended into years of chaos.

In 1994 Clinton came under tremendous attack for inaction in the face of the genocide in Rwanda. Our foreign policy was, it seemed to me, almost disengaged. However, I was more supportive than not of this caution. I felt it was impractical for the United States to become engaged, militarily, in various local conflicts around the world, but especially in Africa, a continent far removed from American consciousness. The Cold War seemed to be over and the United States, at that time, had continued to object to characterizations that it serve as world policeman. Indeed, the notion that the United States could not be the world's policeman seemed to be a basic tenet of U.S. foreign policy to the end of the millennium. Sometime after that, it was quietly reversed.

Richard Holbrooke had left Germany and become assistant secretary for Europe, and John Kornblum, who had been my first boss in Berlin, was his principal deputy. Holbrooke's office was across the hall from my own. I became the designated "Bosnia crisis" person, from inside the NATO office, to work with the Bosnia team. This entailed a large amount of brainstorming, and trying to keep up with the twists and turns of an immensely complex crisis, in which the United States was only starting to get involved. To my mind, Holbrooke had a gift of always knowing where the moral high ground was, and he staked it out clearly in July 1995, in his outrage over the Srebrenica massacre.

Part of working the Bosnia crisis entailed always being available at any time, for any task that Holbrooke or Kornblum could think of. I recall long hours sitting in Holbrooke's office after work, with a half-dozen other State Department people, chewing over Bosnia. About a week or two after Srebrenica, Holbrooke was ranting with rage over the murders. He turned to all of us seated in the room and asked us "What should we do now?" Diplomats hate giving the wrong answers in these situations, especially to someone as unforgiving as Holbrooke, so most answers usually entailed a little bit of this and little bit of that. But to this question, as most of us gazed at the ceiling, one rather junior officer in the meeting suddenly spoke up with a single phrase full of conviction: "Bomb them." What an undiplomatic approach, I thought to myself. Holbrooke gazed at the rest of us, but heard nothing else. He acknowledged the suggestion to bomb. No one objected. Holbrooke asked his assistant to get the Pentagon chief of military operations on the phone. When the general was on the line, Holbrooke said "General, I have an officer here who wants us to bomb the Bosnian Serbs. How do we do it?" That call was the first step.

Over the next few weeks, we put together a strategy to get to the point of bombing, using NATO assets in Italy. My office was responsible for sending instructions to our ambassador at NATO, Robert Hunter, and seeking NATO Council approval of the plans. These were achieved relatively easily. During this period, Holbrooke and others were traveling around the Balkans trying to triangulate diplomatic solutions, with the background rumbling of possible NATO action.

Suddenly, on August 19, the U.S. press began reporting that several U.S. diplomats had been killed in a road accident on Mount Igman out of Sarajevo. As it turned out, the unfortunate victims included Robert Frasure, one of Holbrooke's deputy assistant secretaries, and a person with whom I had been chatting regularly just prior to the accident. Holbrooke had been traveling with the group at the time, when one of their two armored personnel carriers (APC) lost its footing on the road and tumbled over the side several hundred feet, before bursting into flames. Holbrooke was in the other APC. The entire Bosnia team in Washington traveled to Andrews Air Force Base shortly thereafter to honor the return of the three who were killed. It was a stirring moment of reflection that nonetheless contributed to the increasing effect the conflict was having on all of us. I wondered at the time if this would take our diplomacy in a more disengaged direction. Quite the opposite, in fact. Things continued to gather speed.

At one point, it was explained internally to a few of us, that we were waiting a bit with the planned military air strikes to first allow a summertime Croatian offensive against the Serbs to pick up steam and push the Serbs back a bit. The Bosnia team seemed to be watching for some kind of balance of forces over ethnic regions to be established. It seemed that a ceasefire of any kind would only work once the Serbs were back on their heels.

As tensions mounted in August 1995 about possible military action, we were told that Deputy Secretary of State Strobe Talbott wanted to ensure that he had a direct link to the Pentagon and NATO, when NATO bombing started. I was selected for the task of sitting in the State Operations Center the night bombing began. I reported the first wave of bombers, when launched, to Talbott and others. What was striking in hindsight, was the sense that this was Holbrooke's air campaign, and he really was in charge of it. The Pentagon was doing his bidding.

Operation Deliberate Force took place between August 30 and September 20, 1995. Early on, targets largely included communication nodes and antennas belonging to the Bosnia Serbs. However, pilots also had orders to hit any Serb tanks and artillery they observed. Nevertheless, after just a few days of bombing, military planners began to complain that they were running out of targets. It was very hard to locate unconcealed tanks or other larger targets. At one point, we brought a map into Holbrooke's office and began pointing at things that might make good targets. Perhaps most revealing, I do not recall a single report of a single human death as a result of the bombings. Despite lots of sorties and bombs, it seemed to be an air campaign with very little collateral damage. In many ways, U.S. policy in those years seemed to be defined by a definitive premium of avoiding loss of life in any conflict, and never putting U.S. ground troops in harm's way.

In late August we had a pause of several days in the bombings. I understood at the time that this was the result of Holbrooke's desire to demonstrate serious intentions in his own talks at that point with the Serbs and to show that he could turn the bombing on and off, at will. During much of this time, Holbrooke was in the region working to negotiate some arrangement for the Serbs to back down from their threats to the U.N. safe areas.

By early September, Holbrooke's principal deputy, John C. Kornblum, summoned me to his office and asked me out of the blue to begin drafting two papers: one on what role international civilian officials might play implementing a peace agreement; the other, working with the Pentagon, on the military aspects of any peace deal. In the midst of the bombing, Kornblum was taking it upon himself to piece together the components of what would be needed in the event we ever reached a peace agreement. It seemed very premature.

After failing at one draft of civilian implementation of a peace arrangement, I quickly produced a paper that sailed to the Principal's Committee (cabinet) and was approved with praise despite it being only a concept. In the early drafts, I designated the chief civilian official as the "senior coordinator," who would liaise

with NGOs and military officials to coordinate non-military stabilization activities in Bosnia after a ceasefire. Acronyms are important, so I tagged the official "SECOR," for senior coordinator. As
the concept was subsequently talked up among allies, the French
became upset by the acronym, for apparently suggesting insuffi-
cient clout, and after protesting to the National Security Council,
the acronym was changed to the High Representative, which it
remained for decades after the peace.

Work on the military plan was more constrained as the Pentagon owned most resources for military planning. The concept for a
military role, post-ceasefire, remained a work in progress that was
constantly updated as the situation on the ground evolved. The key
element to the military part, however, was to authorize deployed
troops to shoot at will, without having to check with headquarters commanders or political leaders first. This had been the fatal
lesson of Srebrenica, when Bosnian Serb forces simply walked in
and overran Dutch peacekeepers, who did not have permission
from the United Nations to shoot. This would not happen to U.S.
forces.

Kornblum had asked a half-dozen others to also contribute
papers on various aspects of what a peace construct might look like.
These included a draft on elections, a constitution, police, refugees,
and human rights. The people working these papers created them
out of whole cloth, based on what they felt would work best in a
post-conflict Bosnia. Kornblum's concept was to produce a "general
framework" agreement, with a dozen or so annexes addressing
specific aspects of broader peace accord. Holbrooke was in the
field negotiating the conflict, while Kornblum was quietly drafting
the peace in Washington. It was an inspired moment in diplomatic

history.

The bombing ended on September 20, after Holbrooke secured agreement of all parties to travel to Dayton, Ohio, in November, to negotiate a peace deal. The terms of that agreement were left to the negotiations in Dayton. By that time, however, we already had a document of more than 120 pages ready to present in Dayton.

The agreement to attend Dayton was a turning point, and all of a sudden the scent of success began to breed many fathers. Instructions from the top of the State Department were handed down that the Bosnia team was to find key jobs in the effort for several top political appointees, who were looking for something to do. These appointees would then go with Holbrooke to Dayton and negotiate any remaining details. I was instructed by Kornblum to take all the work I had done on civilian implementation, carry it down the hall, and transfer it completely to Robert Gallucci, who was then tasked with negotiating the text with the warring parties when negotiations started. It was not a happy day. Though dictated from top levels of the State Department, I felt robbed of a great project for which others would now take credit. Still, I continued to have a piece of the military action.

In November, large numbers of people traveled to Dayton for the talks. Serb leader Milošević, Croatian president Tudjman, and Bosnian president Izetbegovic were there for extended periods. The Bosnian Serbs were represented within the Milosevic delegation. Holbrooke, Kornblum, and the Bosnia team were there running things. The approach seemed to be to drop the document on the parties and get them to sign. All the leaders were "locked" inside

Wright-Patterson Air Force Base, in Dayton. Each delegation had its own building so that it would not have to directly interact with its enemies. Holbrooke would commute between buildings and extract compromises as needed. The weather and setting were so dismal, that no one planned for the Balkan leaders to stay long. Virtually none of the Americans wanted to stay any longer than was necessary.

At one point, toward the end of the talks, when things stalled, Holbrooke instructed all of us to pack our bags and put them out in front our building the following morning since we were going to end the talks. He was having trouble getting the parties to agree to the text. Some hoped a departure would really happen. I was becoming dizzy with exhaustion. However, the bags sat outside all day and were then brought back to our rooms as talks resumed.

However, the Balkan leaders surprised everyone. They seemed in no hurry to finalize an agreement. They seemed to like the Dayton air base. Some of us speculated that they seemed to relish the (cafeteria-style) food and the cable TV, and hence were in no rush to return back to the war. For the U.S. delegation, this was unsettling, given the drabness of Dayton and endless work hours during an exceptionally cold November.

I spent the final two weeks at Dayton, which was an eternity. I had never been so tired in my life, as the negotiations went on around the clock with tweaks and redrafts of the document constantly being made. Many reached a point where they could only think of getting home to bed, whether or not agreement to the document was ever achieved. It was never entirely clear to me what was happening at any given time. Many of us spent the days lingering in the small office rooms, waiting for things to do or coming up with new twists of phrase.

At one point, toward the end, we were all working until after 4 a.m. Everyone was a zombie. Holbrooke called the team together and said we could go get some sleep, but to be back for a full staff meeting at 6 a.m., a scant two hours later. At 6 a.m., a bedraggled group gathered around the U.S. conference table. Secretary of State Warren Christopher came into the room impeccably adorned in a vested, dark pinstripe suit, sporting gold cuff links, and looking chipper and alert. At the same time, Holbrooke wandered barefoot into the room wearing a T-shirt with wet, uncombed hair. Not an eyebrow was raised to suggest anything amiss. It was classic Holbrooke. He conducted the meeting with focus, as usual, oblivious to the stunning contrast between himself and Christopher.

On the final day, Holbrooke announced that he had agreement of the parties to the document, and we would have a signing ceremony in a few hours. He asked people to begin reading the peace agreement text for errors of any kind. With so many hands in the pot, it was hard controlling any one master document. Given that it was some 120 pages of complexity, on numerous issues, it was challenging for any one person to comprehend. I was still not sure anyone had actually read the entire thing. Indeed, less than an hour before the signing, there was a mad panic when someone realized we had overlooked any resolution of a problem pertaining to the status of the city of Brcko. A quick fix was designed on a whim and inserted without any further negotiation and the document continued forward.

Milošević, Tudjman, and Izetbegovic marched into the

conference room separately, each flanked by supersized bodyguards in black leather coats. There was not a smile to be found. They

SECRETARY OF STATE WARREN CHRISTOPHER & THE AUTHOR IN WASHINGTON, APRIL 1996

solemnly took their places at a signing table, and without words or acknowledgment of the others, signed the document. It suddenly was a heady moment. However, none of us seemed completely sure that the agreement would necessarily last more than a few weeks. The successful signing seemed to surprise all. I flew back to Washington with a tired but happy crowd on Christopher's plane. Escape.

In the subsequent months, I was asked to then turn my attention to implementation of Annex 1b of the agreement. That annex dealt with regional stabilization and arms control. In fact, the idea was to get the tanks and artillery out of the hands of the Bosnian Serbs in a managed way, under the auspices of the Organization for Security and Cooperation in Europe, and eventually destroyed.

I was asked to lead the talks for the United States to this end. It was a task that took some time.

In January 1997 I traveled to Vienna for a meeting with the Serbs, Bosniaks, and Croats on implementation of the annex. Expectations were not high. History had few examples of forces surrendering their weapons freely or easily. The Bosnian Serbs sent as their chief negotiator, Zdravko Tolimir, who was a deputy to Bosnian Serb Ratko Mladic, who had been in charge of the Srebrenica massacre. (Note: In 2007, Tolimir was indicted for war crimes by the International Criminal Tribunal for the Former Yugoslavia, ICTY. He was convicted of genocide on December 12, 2012, and is serving a life sentence in The Hague.) I had always found the Bosnian Serbs a rather scary crowd to deal with. Tolimir was no exception.

At the introductory reception for the OSCE meeting, I wandered over to Tolimir, who was standing alone. I knew that he spoke only Russian and Serb, and for this reason few people could communicate with him. So I began chatting with him in Russian. He responded as if I was the only person he could actually communicate with. After some minor chitchat, I emphasized to him the importance of the Vienna meeting. I then went on to reminisce to him about the night we decided in Holbrooke's office to bomb the Bosnian Serbs. I made it sound easy. I tried to leave the notion that it could happen again if the Bosnian Serbs remained uncooperative on surrendering their weapons to OSCE inspectors. Tolimir listened, smiled politely, but said little. I went on to say that I wanted him to come to the meeting the next day and agree to surrender his tanks and heavy artillery to the OSCE. I emphasized that I was demanding that he do this and that it needed to be done within 24 hours. No more delays were appropriate. It was not normal diplomacy. Bluffing was risky. Holbrooke's tactics were infecting us all.

The next day, Tolimir invited me to a private chat. He was absolutely polite and chatty. A different person, almost. We sat down and he said he was working on my suggestion. He asked if I had ever visited the Bosnian Serb stronghold of Pale. I said no. He said he would like to invite me to visit him in Pale. He noted that there was skiing. I said that was very nice, but I still wanted him to surrender his weapons.

Within hours, the Bosnian Serbs announced that they were willing to surrender their tanks and heavy artillery to OSCE inspectors for disposal. It was a sudden and surprising break-through. When I arrived back in Washington a day or two later, people were stunned at the unexpected concession. Washington had received multiple reports, suddenly, that the Serbs had agreed on weapons disposal, and were surprised that my talk with Tolimir produced this concession. It was a rare diplomatic moment—and I, too, was speechless.

Two months later, Tolimir was fired from his Serb military duties. We were not sure why he lost his job. Nevertheless, we worked hard to hold the Bosnian Serbs to Tolimir's commitment on weapons destruction. Indeed, the Bosnian Serb prime minister traveled to Washington in spring 1997 for a meeting with Assis-tant Secretary John Kornblum and to assert that the disarmament agreement was flawed. Kornblum called me to the meeting to verify the details of the deal with the Serbs, and the prime minister finally relented in a huff. Several months later, OSCE inspectors began destroying the Bosnian Serb tanks and artillery that had besieged Sarajevo for so long.

The years working on Bosnia were in many ways some of the most meaningful of my career, but they wore down most of those who were at the heart of the effort. Almost every single diplomatic officer who invested round-the-clock work in the effort during those days wound up leaving the State Department within a year or two. Some commented to me, "There must be more to life than this." The work had been all consuming, tedious, and physically demanding to the point of total exhaustion. I sit in awe of every colleague from those efforts. Each of them was gifted.

CHAPTER ELEVEN

DUCK POND REVISITED

(1997)

P resident Clinton won well-deserved credit for the Dayton Peace Agreement. It provided a convincing foreign-policy success after a first term that was otherwise anemic in foreign affairs. The United States, in a very short time, had contributed to the withdrawal of the nuclear threat in Europe (INF Agreement), the unification of Germany, the withdrawal of the Red Army from eastern Europe, the warming of relations with Moscow, and a peaceful outcome in Bosnia with no U.S. military lost. It felt successful.

As I gazed into my favorite duck pond in July 1997, nibbling on another peanut butter and jelly sandwich, I felt that diplomacy had become much more operational than I would have originally anticipated. It seemed we were spending less and less time chewing over visions of global governance, Realpolitik, and security structures, while devoting ever more energy to local conflicts. This bothered me. In my early diplomatic years, I recall lengthy discussions about "visions" for policy. It was critical in the 1980s and 1990s to have a "concept" for where we were headed. These kinds of visions were important signposts for incorporating our values into our goals. Values such as democracy, independence, freedom, tolerance, listening, comprehending, and sharing, were essential in the bipolar world and beyond. But we had always been taught in school that if bipolarity broke down, the clarity of those values would go out of focus. Strategic visions were necessary, in my view, to keep the values alive. Somewhere toward the end of the millennium, that contemplative aspect to diplomacy gave way to the operational implementation of tasks.

I watched that year's group of teenage ducklings circling around the pond, eyeing me with a plea for some breadcrumbs. My family would be displeased if I did not share. But I don't recall if I did.

I wandered back up toward the State Department, amazed at the majesty of Washington and the effect that power had on people. I was not excluded. Ambition and drive compelled one to do what the masters wished, while at the same time trying to impress with savvy intelligence and wittiness. The Bosnia team had been good. I was not sure I could keep up at that level. I bid farewell to the ducklings and ambled off toward another sojourn overseas.

CHAPTER TWELVE

MUNICH CONSUL GENERAL

(1997)

After the tribulations of the Bosnia effort, I was sent to Munich. The post of consul general in Munich was different from all previous assignments. It was a bit of a reward for the Bosnia experience. It was one of America's largest consulates, with more than 140 employees, in one of the world's most fashionable cities. It also levied a premium on form over substance. It was most enjoyable in almost every respect, but largely ignored by Washington in terms of policy.

Edmund Stoiber was the governor of Bavaria during my time in Munich. A gangling and gregarious politician, he was the strongman of his state and a rising politician on the national scene. The headline issue upon my arrival was what to do with the Amerika Haus, a cultural center remnant of the postwar period when Washington worked hard to influence thinking around Germany. Such centers were platforms for explaining U.S. priorities and the American way of life to a newly born Federal Republic of Germany. They were immensely popular as symbols of the U.S. commitment to Germany and its people. However, after German

BAVARIAN GOVERNOR EDMUND STOIBER AND
CONSUL GENERAL GLASS IN MUNICH 1999

unification, Washington began to unwind all the "legacy" components of the special nature of U.S.-German postwar relations. In
fact, the end of the Cold War actually provided the United States
with a chance to slowly turn away from Germany to some degree,
almost as if it were becoming yesterday's beer. Cultural centers
such as Amerika Haus fell one by one to the budget axe.

As the new consul general, I was left with the news that the
United States was withdrawing financial support for the Amerika
Haus in Munich. We were withdrawing not just some financial
support, but all financial support. As a convinced Atlanticist, I was
thoroughly aghast. Was Germany no longer a critical ally? How
were we to continue preaching freedom and democracy? Luckily,
the Bavarian government was among the most U.S.-friendly groups
to be found in the world. Edmund Stoiber's government worked
diligently and generously with me, over several months, to develop

a transition plan for the Amerika Haus building in downtown Munich. In the end, the Bavarians agreed to contribute well over $500,000 a year to the continued survival of the institution. The United States, as a partner in the effort, would "contribute" program-ming and speakers to fill the place with activity. It was remarkable generosity in my view, and reflec-tive of the special feelings Bavarians harbored for Americans.

At the consulate, we worked hard over the ensuing years to bring speakers, authors, and other experts to the building for public events. We tried to build audiences and supporters. I delivered speech after speech on freedom, individuality, and partnership. Nevertheless, it became increasingly difficult to fill

CIA DIRECTOR GEORGE TENET STOPS BY THE MUNICH CONSULATE GENERAL IN LATE 1997

the 500-seat auditorium in the post-unification, post-Cold War environment. Germany was no longer on the front line of global conflict. German reliance on the United States was changing; and the big brother of democracy was no longer so central to the new German identity. Nevertheless, with Bavarian financial assis-tance, we managed to keep Munich's Amerika Haus alive and well through the end of the millennium.

The largest political challenge during my time in Bavaria was dealing with the small community of Holzkirchen. Local activists were demonstrating passionately for the U.S. government to dismantle a U.S. broadcast station and antenna array in the midst of their pastoral farming fields. The station and antennas were owned and operated by the U.S. Broadcasting Board of Governors. They had originally been part of the Cold War operations of Radio Free Europe/Radio Liberty, broadcasting AM signals for years, about freedom and democracy, out of Munich. With the end of the Cold War, local residents began to pound the drums about electronic smog, which they claimed was affecting their health as well as driving their cows mad.

Amid inconclusive studies on the effects of AM transmissions on cow brains, local activists worked themselves into a total frenzy of despair. They utilized local reporters to feed constant criticism of the transmitting station, and created an aura of perceived health threats that were larger than life. They demanded that the U.S. government close the station and absorb a financial loss of some $35 million. I visited with local officials and with local activists, and held press conferences to debunk the growing mythology around Holzkirchen station's effects on cows. I pointed out the critical nature of the station's broadcasting to the Balkans, and how important this remained for Balkan and German stability.

Most Bavarians outside of Holzkirchen could not have cared less about the antennas. Some local pundits speculated that the nearby residents just wanted the land back from the United States and were hoping that the state government would buy out the station. The Stoiber government was acutely sensitive to the issue, ostensibly seeking a solution without siding with either party. By the time of my departure, in 2000, the Holzkirchen station was on sound legal footing, and a good deal of the local political pressure was muted. Nevertheless, the local residents persisted, and during the term of my successor in Munich, they convinced the United States to close the station and antennas. My successor apparently decided the facility was no longer worth the effort.

Consul generals travel a lot around their districts, meeting

CONSUL GENERAL GLASS WELCOMES DEFENSE SECRETARY
WILLIAM COHEN AND SENATOR CARL LEVIN TO MUNICH FOR THE
ANNUAL SECURITY CONFERENCE IN FEBRUARY 1998

local officials, making speeches, and even kissing the occasional baby. I enjoyed this immensely and probably delivered several hundred speeches over the course of three years. Most remarks were about the special character of U.S.-German relations, despite

Washington's growing apathy with such niceties. Others highlighted a technology partnership we were encouraging between Bavaria and California. Meetings with government, industrial, and cultural leaders were uniformly warm and friendly.

At the same time, it was important to recognize that these years were a golden age of U.S. diplomacy (much like Japan in the 1980s), and perhaps the best time to work as a diplomat. The U.S. economy was booming as the technology bubble was inflating spectacularly in the United States. Foreigners believed that the United States had found some magic formula, economically, and thus we frequently showcased visiting U.S. executives for their particular audience appeal. Business leaders such as Microsoft's Bill Gates and Sun's Scott McNealy occasionally visited their operations in Munich, which had become Germany's equivalent of Silicon Valley, at least in the minds of the Bavarians. Indeed, one of Stoiber's highest priorities was promoting the U.S. "technology partnership."

L TO R: CONSUL GENERAL GLASS, DEFENSE SECRETARY WILLIAM COHEN, AMBASSADOR JOHN C. KORNBLUM IN MUNICH IN FEBRUARY 1998

At the same time, the United States was glowing in the wake of foreign policy successes in Dayton and Kosovo. It appeared that we had assumed leadership in crises, and were the horse to bet on. Peering into the U.S. paradigm of the future was easier than ever at this juncture. Even the bombing of the U.S. embassies in Africa did not set back U.S. leadership. We responded with missile retaliation. We also quietly found and dealt with key perpetrators. Indeed, one of the central people responsible for the bombings in Africa was arrested in Bavaria and extradited to the United States, where he was convicted and imprisoned in New York State. The Bavarian role in assisting with this was extremely cooperative and discrete.

During this period, John Kornblum was ambassador to Germany, one of few career officers (not political appointee) to ever hold the position. His unparalleled knowledge of German and Germany provided a unique strength to U.S. policy in Europe at its zenith. He held the line well against apathy in Washington, but the sands of history were shifting eastward. Germany was the "front" during the Cold War and the unification phase; but it became "old Europe" in the face of the east European members of NATO that started arriving in 1999.

At one point I received word that Richard Holbrooke, who was now working outside of government, planned to visit Munich. I immediately did what any diplomat would do: I put together a large luncheon in his honor and invited every VIP I could find in the region. Holbrooke was always good value, and, as he was volatile and always in the midst of something, I anticipated a bit of drama. The day before the luncheon I went to meet briefly with him. He regaled me with tales of his recent sojourns around Africa. He shared with me anecdotes of his meetings with several African presidents, one of whom was preparing for a new war that would kill thousands. Holbrooke recounted that this certain president had been boasting to him that all of his country's troops wanted to die for him; that the war would start in days. He showed me a silver crown he had picked up locally for his wife. He was in his element.

The next day, I was preparing the luncheon at my house for a swarm of excited guests when I received a call from Holbrooke thirty minutes prior to the event. He asked me whether he really had to come to the lunch. He had other things to do. As the blood drained from my face and dizziness set in, I told him he absolutely had to be there. It was critical (at least for me). He showed up with his enigmatic ways in full display. Showing up is the largest part of many diplomatic challenges.

Toward the end of 1999, the consulate organized a very large conference for companies and officials on the issue of Y2K, the renowned computer glitch that was supposed to catalyze massive computer failure on January 1, 2000. Over two days we hosted renowned intellectuals, such as Bill Joy, from the U.S. tech scene, and included other key economists speaking on technological development. It was an inspired time. At the turn of the millennium, life was promising in Bavaria; and no Y2K glitches struck. I had filled my bathtub with water just in case, but the old millennium ended on a very, very high note. It seemed like things could only improve.

CHAPTER THIRTEEN

BERN: MONEY & FAMILY
(2000)

In late summer 2000, I moved on to become deputy chief of mission in Switzerland. The ambassador, J. Richard Fredericks, was a political appointee who had worked as an investment analyst prior to his new assignment. He was renowned for having made lots of money, and I seem to recall he was rumored to have been a roommate of Bill Clinton's at one point. During one of my early trips to introduce myself to the ambassador, I was enticed to participate in several hours of go-kart racing at a track in Switzerland. I was terrified of whizzing around a track at uncontrollable speeds and occasionally crashing into others, but I did my duty and survived toward the back of the pack. The ambassador was a friendly and gregarious gentleman who was doggedly determined to be liked by everyone, at any cost, a most common ailment that infected appointees unsure of their new careers.

Every job at the State Department has different demands, many of which are unpredictable. However, the longer one is in the Service, the more the chasm between career and family seems to take over. This is something many of us face in very different ways. Bern was my first conflict. The very day I departed Philadelphia for the new job in Switzerland, I had to abandon my mother, alone in her small New Jersey home. My father had died four years prior, and I was an only child. My mother was now extremely and seriously ill, and could not drive. I was her only living relative. But travel plans to Switzerland had been made. It was the last time I would see her outside of a hospital.

Switzerland was, of course, dripping with beauty. Nevertheless, it was an unusual country, almost a complete backwater, for a diplomat. Outside of the EU and NATO, Switzerland was not part of any larger security or economic structures that were of any interest to Washington. The fact that it had an extremely decentralized government, and a rotating presidency, meant that it was difficult to obtain firm government support for action on anything of any consequence. The name of the game in Switzerland during my year was to encourage commercial and financial interaction, and seek any cooperation possible in the effort to combat money laundering. This goal was accomplished largely by holding small conferences that included banking and government contacts whenever Washington experts on money laundering passed through the country. Swiss banks were very difficult to engage, but these were the first days of pressing for greater collaboration with the United States, against the bad guys. It was only marginally interesting. Swiss interlocutors made all the right noises about cooperation, but behind the scenes clung to bank secrecy as if it was their lifeblood.

In less than two months, I found myself suddenly on the way back to New Jersey after my 73-year-old mother had suffered several heart attacks and was very unstable in intensive care. I had just been promoted to the Senior Foreign Service, but the joy was subdued. As the only child, and only close relative, it was extremely difficult for me. I arrived at her bedside to find her half-conscious. The doctors were not sure what was happening, as she had no prior history of heart problems. After several days, they transferred her to Philadelphia, where she grudgingly agreed to heart bypass surgery. It was a tough operation. She barely survived the surgery, and the surgeon confided to me that he had almost lost her at one point. I commuted to Philadelphia daily from her house in New Jersey. She was making good progress for about a week until, suddenly, one day I arrived at the hospital to find her back on a life-support ventilator, with breathing problems. It was a major setback, though the doctors shrugged it off. I continued to visit, and her situation was relatively stable but not improving.

Having been away from my new job for several weeks, I began to feel the professional need to return to Switzerland. The doctors indicated it could be weeks or months before my mother's situation changed. I was more torn than ever in life, as I was the only relative to visit her or care for her at this point. I made the decision to return to Switzerland, opting for career over family, though my mother signaled that she supported the decision. As I stood there dabbing water on my mother's lips to the eerie sound of the pulmonary ventilator, I was overwhelmed with guilt, convinced in my heart that returning to Switzerland was wrong. It was.

In Switzerland I was totally distracted, calling the hospital every day. Two weeks later, the doctors called to report that my mother was not improving and they were increasingly unsure she ever would. They said they could continue to keep her alive by intervening every time her heart acted up. They asked, however, "how much intervention" I wanted them to perform. I agreed to a middle path of less intervention, haunted by the sense of abandoning my family. Several days later, my mother died after a visit by her pastor. I rushed back to New Jersey to organize a service and funeral. After that, I gathered up all her possessions, donated most to charity and put the rest in storage. I then had her house repainted and repaired inside and out, before putting it on the market. After another month, I returned to Switzerland. My year was passing by without my presence in the embassy. In early January, I required hospitalization myself in Bern. Recuperation took several weeks. This added to the challenge of being on the job.

By mid-March 2001, I began reaping criticism from the staff for having ignored the embassy, as I had not been around enough even to invite the staff to my home for the obligatory housewarming reception. Over the next month, I endeavored to overcome this deficit with receptions and outreach to the staff. Things began to improve nicely. However, the political calendar did not help. The 2000 presidential election in the United States signaled that the ambassador needed to start packing his bags in May for departure. He did not want to go. He was on the phone to anyone he could think of to try to find a way to stay in Switzerland, with his banking friends. His successor was in the works, and every ambassador made changes, especially after such a hotly contested presidential election. I did not fare well that year, and I decided to depart post after one year and return to Washington. Switzerland was not working out. I had not even seen the mountains. I left with a feeling of having betrayed my family and my career—something more common than not among my diplomatic colleagues. It left an extremely bitter aftertaste.

WASHINGTON: SANCTIONS & TERROR

(2001)

After extended home leave, I arrived back in Washington in early September 2001. The State Department was unsure of what I would do next; they frequently leave it up to the officer to shop around for a new assignment, walking the halls in the off chance that you will run into someone with a job to offer. After only four days, while savoring the new Starbuck's operation in the basement café, I stumbled across Assistant Secretary for Economics Tony Wayne. We had known each other fleetingly since Bosnia days in the European bureau. After a brief chat, he told me to look into the job of director of sanctions in his bureau. Within a few days I interviewed for the job with Deputy Assistant Secretary Anna Borg, one of the best managers I've ever met, and was assigned. I had no idea what was expected. I was not an economist, knew nothing about sanctions, did not really want to learn mundane issues, and was a political officer.

Then September 11 occurred. I was driving down the Cabin John Parkway to the State Department that morning, listening to the radio reports of a plane crashing into the Twin Towers. At first it was just one report of one small plane. Then came a report of a second plane. As I got closer to the State Department, traffic was noticeably worse. I parked and began to walk toward the back door D Street entrance to the building, while at the same time noticing a curious, large black plume of smoke rising in the distance from the direction of the Pentagon. I had no idea what that was.

I managed to get inside the back entrance to the building, when alarms began shrieking throughout the corridors in a way I had never experienced before. Suddenly employees came sprinting full-tilt out of the building, some vaulting over the entrance turnstiles to get out fast. I immediately turned around and went back outside the building with the chilling sense that we were under direct attack and no one knew where the next hit would be. I kept looking to the sky wondering if another plane would target the State Department. The distinct feeling of being under attack was more real than I've ever experienced. I quickly returned to my car and managed to get back out of town to my family in Maryland.

Terrorist Finance

I began my new position as director of sanctions within days. However, 9/11 had changed everything. Almost from day one, Tony Wayne and I were attending daily interagency meetings at the Treasury Department to devise new ways to combat terrorism. The idea was to freeze terrorist finances everywhere, and fast. Because the Treasury Department was responsible for most economic and financial sanctions levied by the United States, it emerged as the lead agency to stop terrorist finance. My office provided the foreign policy direction for these efforts, namely, lining up other countries to freeze assets with us. On September 24, 2001, President Bush announced the first "list" of names of terrorists whose assets were being immediately frozen in the United States. The list included the name bin Laden.

The U.S. government had never embarked on asset freezes of individual terrorists before. However, there had been some limited experience freezing the assets of drug kingpins and rogue nations. Under the International Emergency Economic Powers Act of 1977, the president had the power to issue executive orders to all financial institutions, requiring them to freeze specified assets. It only started to use this authority in a substantial fashion after 9/11. Over a dozen agencies began meeting up to several times a week at Treasury or the White House, to begin identifying the terrorists and their supporters, and then acting to freeze their assets indefinitely. Treasury General Counsel David Aufhauser led the effort at Treasury; Jody Powell led the effort for the National Security Council.

It was absorbing to see the representatives of all the agencies gather to discuss who could be tougher on terrorism. There was understandably only one side of discussion, and that was being tough. The State Department was generally viewed as excessively soft when it came to hard power and terrorism; we were supposed to "protect" international sensitivities. No one was particularly concerned with due process or civil rights, as there was an understanding that we were treading unprecedented turf. I often wondered in those days how hard it would be to press for moderation amid the thundering war on terror. I never found out. Even the lawyers in the room, of which there were plenty, were focused only on how to justify whatever actions we wanted to take.

Perhaps, this microcosm of U.S. policymaking dynamics underlay the robust and increasingly shrill demeanor of the United States, on an international scale, in those years. Somewhat encouraging, however, was the almost unquestioned support we received at the United Nations and around the world for our efforts.

We realized that financial assets were fungible and that simply freezing them in the United States was but a small part of the battle. We needed to use the United Nations and our diplomatic relations to also compel other countries to act. And it all had to be done at the same time, by all, to prevent money from "escaping." Within a few weeks, my office developed a system of reporting accounts about to be frozen by Washington to the U.N. Sanctions Committee in New York, for expeditious approval for immediate freezing by all U.N. member

STATE DEPARTMENT ASSISTANT SECRETARY FOR ECONOMICS E. ANTHONY WAYNE, GEORGE GLASS, TREASURY DEPARTMENT DIRECTOR OF OFFICE OF FOREIGN ASSETS CONTROL (OFAC) RICHARD NEWCOMB IN 2004

states. Though the process worked better in theory than practice, over time it provided substantial leverage to press countries around the world to hunt down and seize assets belonging to terrorists and affiliated organizations within a 48-hour window.

We began producing list after list of persons and organizations to designate for asset freezes, and President Bush dutifully announced many of these actions. It became one of the newest and most innovative aspects of the war on terror. My office was re-designated the Office of Terrorist Finance and Sanctions. We began running training courses for diplomats, on how to manage terrorist finance operations in countries around the world. More than $140 million of terrorist assets were frozen within a matter of weeks, more than one-third of it in Europe.

The challenge to the program was having sufficient information to identify potential selectees for addition to the lists, which became public knowledge at the time of designation by the White House. People and governments wanted evidence of terrorist affiliation and support. But the classified nature of intelligence made it impossible to pursue every case all the way into the courtroom. In the early days, the process was highly challenged by a paucity of useful information. Over time, this improved as the entire U.S. government massively shifted attention and resources to terrorism.

Still, in the early days, at one point we designated one Mohammed Zia with little additional information. The problem was that there were several million people in Pakistan with this name. Identifying the correct person required greater precision, which was simply not available. Also problematic at the time was identifying precise members of the Taliban. Afghanis routinely did not have or even know their own birthdays. Documentation of any kind was sparse. I spent long hours poring over fragments of information trying to find ways to identify individual Taliban members, but with very little success. It was difficult to ask the United Nations to designate terrorists if we were unable to be sure who they were or how a bank should identify them. Still, with persistence the effort took on steam into the middle of the decade.

During the same period, just after 9/11, my office received an early draft of what later became the Patriot Act legislation. Congressional staffers provided the draft for informal, advance views from various government agencies, which also provided an opportunity for agencies to add things to the legislation. At the time, I had the impression that Congress was simply looking for a way to get in the game and was offering to give the administration whatever it wanted legislatively to combat terrorism. No harm in that. Or was there?

Nonetheless, within a few days we were provided a "final" draft of the legislation for any comments we might have within 24 hours. I asked one of my lawyers to review the very lengthy and complex document. He said he reviewed it but had no partic- ular reaction to the text. I recall thinking that it was so complex that it would be difficult to know what any of it would mean in practice. But everything was short term in the aftermath of 9/11, and it would take a long time to understand the implications of the Patriot Act. By then it could be changed if necessary. Perhaps Congress was thinking the same way. The counterterrorism train was already leaving the station. We would correct any errors later.

Iraq War Preparations

As 2002 rolled along, the discussion of Iraq increased. Extra scrutiny was added to any possible nexus of Iraq with terror- ism. However, no connection of any significance emerged, in my view, in the terrorist finance world. By late 2002 and early 2003, it became increasingly clear that we might engage in hostilities with Iraq. However, the State Department seemed to be outside of the decision-making circle, unlike the case in Bosnia.

Assistant Secretary Wayne reported to the staff one day that he had been offering to decision-makers to assist with postwar planning for Iraq on a contingency basis. He noted that, after a conflict, there would be a great need for rebuilding the economy, getting oil facilities working, and building new infrastructure. However, Wayne acknowledged to us that no one seemed interested in this planning assistance. Still, he asked people in the bureau to conduct some limited planning so that we were prepared, in the event it was needed. It was a moment that was indicative of how much the military, alone, seemed to be planning this war.

At one meeting with several other State Department bureaus, we began discussing what to do in the wake of possible hostilities. Some of us recalled that the key to success in Bosnia in 1995 had been the creation of limited "secure areas" in the country, where normal life could resume after the war. We had gathered up weapons and tried to deploy troops, at least on a limited basis, to ensure a degree of order. The response from those leading the meeting was that Iraq was not Bosnia and the new administration "wanted nothing to do with Bosnia." I was stunned. Politics dictated rejecting out of hand any lessons from the past. There was no further discussion of the lessons of Bosnia. At that point, I became skeptical that any planning was taking place. Indeed, one officer respected for his Middle East expertise was transferred to career exile after producing a detailed plan for post-conflict Iraq. State Department input to any postwar planning effort was unwelcome.

Given my office responsibilities for Iraq sanctions, we came to have a growing, albeit marginal role in preparations for the Iraq war. The United States had very strict legislation in place, for example, that prevented us (or others) from legally introducing certain items into Iraq. On close scrutiny, these items included such things as chlorine tablets (chlorine being a precursor for chemical weapons) to purify water, and atropine injectors (to combat the effects of chemical weapons). As any international forces going into Iraq, and non-governmental organizations (NGOs) in their wake, would need these items to survive, we had to coordinate lifting sanctions with the commencement of hostilities.

At one point I was asked to go to the Pentagon to brief the Excomm (the NSC-led Executive Committee planning the war) on the sanctions issues. It was a straightforward briefing. I entered the room to brief the group, only to find some 35 uniformed military. There were two people from the NSC running the meeting, and two people from the State Department, Debra Cagan and Andrew Goodman, as liaisons. What was striking to me was the abundance of uniformed military compared to civilians. It was the opposite of Bosnia. I delivered my briefing, and then was quickly escorted out. That was unusual. It was a very closed group and most State officials were not to be trusted.

On the eve of hostilities, I questioned a colleague in the State Department about the reliability of the intelligence on WMD in Iraq. He emphasized to me over and over that he knew exactly where everything was, and claimed that we were even tracking the movement of WMD around the country—however, he was not permitted to share any details. I remained skeptical until Colin

Powell's U.N. speech in early February 2003. That speech was a turning point for many, including myself. I came to believe that Iraq did possess prohibited WMD and that military action was required. Here was Powell showing pictures of mobile WMD labs, sharing intercepts of phone conversations, and scaring everyone. I was reluctant, but on balance it appeared time to act.

During this period I chaired meetings every week with representatives from most key NGOs, such as the Red Cross, that might be involved in relief efforts after the coming war. Again, the idea here was to ensure that sanctions restrictions did not prohibit their personnel from launching humanitarian operations when the shooting stopped. There was a good deal of planning by these organizations into preparing for large floods of refugees after the fighting. As things turned out, those refugee floods never materialized. As far as I could tell, this was the only area of "planning" done for the coming war. We kept hearing over and over that if we did not win in the first six months, nothing else mattered.

A few weeks before the initiation of hostilities, I was invited to attend a presentation by former Defense Department military planners, who were now working as contractors. In a formal briefing, they provided their best guess as to what would happen in Iraq after the invasion. The presentation with slides and maps was designed for the "Gardner group," the first civilian team going in, on the heels of the troops, to run the country. The briefing was quite detailed and based on decades of military planning experience. The speakers made it crystal clear, over and over, that we would win the battle but lose the war over the longer term. I was shocked that they would say this. They emphasized that the result of the attacks was likely to be long-term incapacitation of the water and electrical systems. They explained, in illustrated detail, how the specific munitions to be used would degrade those systems, thereby making it extremely challenging to restore any of them. They described damage to oil facilities, which would cut off Iraq's revenue stream for years. But their bottom line that, over time, we would not succeed, fell with a deafening thud in the audience.

After the presentation, I never heard again any speculation of what would come after the attack. The only cautionary note making the rounds again was that we had to succeed within the first six weeks. Otherwise, we would lose—whatever that meant. However, within a month of initiation of the war, no one was saying this any longer.

In 2003–2004 we began to refine our terrorist finance efforts. Lawsuits began piling up from companies and businessmen we had "designated" as having supported terrorism. Court cases required evidence, and in many cases this meant classified information, sometimes intelligence. Hence, there was some bureaucratic reluctance to contest individual designations in courts. Most early legal challenges were settled out of court. In most cases, we just removed names from designation lists. I was tasked to travel to Brussels to negotiate with the European Union Commission, and come up with some kind of agreed guidelines for getting names delisted at the United Nations. This was a delicate negotiation as no politician in Washington wanted to appear to even open the door to "going backward" on terrorist designations. Nevertheless, I negotiated a set of procedures with the European Union, and then the U.N. Security Council members. The Security Council adopted those procedures, and the terrorist finance effort continued, albeit with some additional integrity. The Treasury Department earned substantial credit in those years for compelling countries, even in the Middle East, to implement asset freezes. This contributed to a new way of thinking in the world about freezing money that was underwriting terror.

As director of the sanctions office, I also was responsible for responding to requests from the Treasury Department's Office of Foreign Assets Control (OFAC) for "guidance" on whether to issue a license to approve certain exceptions to our various sanctions regimes. For example, we would have to sign off on approvals of export of medical devices or bull semen to Iran. Treasury routinely requested State views, which were usually determinative. In one resounding instance, OFAC enforcement ascertained that the oil tanker Essex was steering a course toward the United States to deliver oil that it had been loaded in the Persian Gulf. However, the United States had evidence that the oil was illegal, prewar Iraqi oil that was being smuggled into the United States.

I decided that it would be inconsistent with our sanctions efforts, even illegal, to permit the tanker to enter port in the United States to offload. We managed to keep the tanker at sea for almost four months, in a state of legal limbo. However, after those months, the European owners of the company orchestrated some high-level phone calls to senior levels of the State Department, claiming that I was causing them to lose money by denying permission to offload in the United States. I was instructed, unofficially, by senior officials in the State Department, to agree to license the oil. I grudgingly agreed to the license, and the oil was sold in the United States. Did money trump law? It was another example of a sanctions regime that had exceptions, particularly whenever the sums involved became too large.

The terrorist finance initiative was a stimulating inter-agency effort, which, I believe, contributed soundly to our efforts to drain some of the support from terrorism. It was particularly notable that, in the early days, resources dedicated to counterter-rorism were few. It was not an area to make big careers. However, by 2004 that had changed dramatically, and new bureaucracies were sprouting up everywhere. It was the new growth industry in government. It was the future.

CHAPTER FIFTEEN

DUCK POND FAREWELL

(2004)

My time in Washington was drawing to a close as I again visited my duck pond one last time. The Cold War was a fading memory, and I was not sure where to look into the future. I was uncomfortable with the recent course of foreign policy, but it was hard to talk about openly in Washington in those days.

I thought the Afghanistan incursion was well warranted in the aftermath of 9/11 and the role of the Taliban. At the time, I felt that the operation was carried out well and should have remained primarily military. The evolution of the effort into one of nation building seemed unreal. In the prior millennium I had always had the impression that the United States despised nation building and that Congress would not support such efforts financially. Suddenly we were rebuilding Afghanistan, a country that traditionally had little to do with the United States. I felt strongly that there was no way we were going to remake that country into our own image. They had traditions and cultures we could never comprehend. I reminded myself that even in Bosnia there was no McDonald's after years because of water and infrastructure issues. Talk of rebuilding Afghanistan (and later, Iraq), like Germany and Japan after WWII, were absolute gibberish. Nevertheless, toppling the Taliban and hunting al Qaida was essential.

At the time, I never quite got over the feeling that the Iraq War was a stretch, as it was just not clear that there was an immediate and grave threat to the United States. In 1991, I recalled a buildup of forces lasting more than six months before we went into Kuwait. I never questioned that endeavor and still defend it. But Iraq was rushed. You could not long expect broad support for war if the premises of the war remained classified and questioned. The State Department was totally cut out of any discussion that may have taken place, and this was wrong. Most parts of government responded only to the National Security Council, and would offer the NSC whatever it seemed to want. Going against that flow would simply deprive you of an invitation to the next meeting. Still, was it better to try to effect marginal change from within the boat, or to jump out into the deepest of waters? I was grateful that I was not put in the position of having to make any such decision. I knew it might have led to my first crisis of conscience since joining the State Department, 22 years prior.

During this period, virtually every office of the State Department had a copy of Colin Powell's newest book on leadership on display. He was widely adored by the career Foreign Service because he was perceived as looking out for State interests. He also seemed genuinely nice. Though I never met Powell, I had a hard time comprehending his decision to go along in the rush to war (i.e., try to effect change from within), rather than objecting and making a stand (that would have surely cost him his job). Remaining in the boat only seemed to garner him lame-duck status in the administration. Not an easy position for such a decorated hero.

Fear of terrorism had swept Washington over the previous few years, and I had deep concerns that we had overplayed our response, and not just in Iraq. Even after several years, it was still not clear to me what exactly the new Department of Homeland Security was about. It was too far-reaching of an institution, with personnel from countless, often invisible, and conflicting agencies. It seemed more like a holding organization for a group of sub-organizations. When Homeland Security representatives attended our interagency meetings on terrorism, they rarely had anything to say. It was almost as if they were unsure what their own role should be. The problem was that it was the White House National Security Council, from the top down, that "coordinated" interagency policy efforts, not some new agency. The interagency would not respond to Homeland Security, but rather only to the White House. So I felt it was a rather directionless organization that added to growing complexity: a potpourri of experts with no vision of where to go.

At the same time, the Patriot Act had lots of tidbits buried in it, just waiting to be discovered. Seizing bank assets was one of them. There were others. Some of these might be useful, but they all seemed to constantly bump up against the issues of due process. In school we had the notion of due process drilled into us, and I had firmly believed that no country in the world promoted due process as a virtue to the extent that the United States had. It was simply foundational. But I wondered whether we had overreacted. Had we allowed 9/11 to terrorize the country to the point where we thought of nothing else, where security was paramount over freedom, due process, and individualism? I recalled listening

to college lectures in the 1970s about terrorism, and the emphasis placed on the desire of terrorists to change the fabric of the
countries they targeted. They wanted to destroy freedoms and
replace them with fear and a security state. I remember watching
Europeans deal with this problem in the 1970s and early 1980s.
I was convinced the U.S. commitment to liberty was uncompro-
mising. Still, I was not encouraged that many in government were
thinking in these terms.

Where had the Cold War gone? By now, everyone was writing
off Russia as a basket case. The Red Army had reportedly rusted,
the Russian economy had nothing but oil, and the Russian population was dominated by corruption. A sorry state of affairs, to be
sure. Since 1999 we had opened the doors of NATO to membership by a growing number of former Warsaw Pact countries. The
Russians seemed to choke now and then on this, but we seemed
to calm them with utterings of special relations with Washington. I was truly amazed that Moscow calmly accepted not only
NATO enlargement, but also EU expansion into eastern Europe
and missile defense. For years, I had listened to the Soviets rail at
me about Western encirclement of their country. It had been an
unremitting mantra. And now no one cared? It did not make sense
to me; but on this point I continued to think back to a college
lecture. I had been taught to look at government policies as being
shaped by (1) bureaucratic fighting, (2) personality politics, or
(3) reason. No single component dominated. Of course, with this
paradigm anything was possible.

My last view of the ducklings. They always seemed to live in
a peaceful world. The world of diplomacy was in disarray. I was
not so sure that anything that I was doing was making any differ-

ence in history. I seriously considered leaving the State Department just to do something different. The last few years of watching government lawyers twist the Geneva Convention out of existence (I had been quoting it since childhood, from WWII) in favor of the Law of War, of which I had never heard a thing prior to 2002, was tiring. I was weary of "evidence" that cannot be talked about against people who cannot be identified. Sanctions had certainly exploited a weakness in due process, and I often wondered what an innocent would do if he mistakenly fell victim to sanctions. There was no obvious recourse to fight against sanctions. It seemed like United States had endless enemies now, and that even the allies we had groomed for decades—Germany and France—we had consigned to the trash heap of "old Europe."

Every country goes through rough periods. I never believed that to be the case for the United States. We were special in my mind. I could still sit with my ducklings under the shadow of the Washington Monument and draw inspiration. I used to lecture for years in Germany that America was more of an idea than a country. It was an idea that encompassed the notions of freedom, rugged individualism, due process, diversity, melting pot, enterprise, entrepreneurship, and protection from excessive government. It was founded on the broad consensus of people who aspire to these ideals. Storms would pass, and a new generation of ducklings would be reviewed by visitors to the duck pond.

CHAPTER SIXTEEN

VIENNA: IRAN NUCLEAR THREAT

(2004)

Assignment time came around again and the State Department was in a contest with other agencies in Washington to send as many people as possible to Iraq. It was believed that flooding the theater with people would bring about solutions, much as flooding the country with soldiers would bring about stability. Most State Department officers were sent to Iraq with virtually no language ability or knowledge of the region. They were also sent without guns. Of course State had a number of experts on Iraq in its own ranks, but these numbers were quickly depleted, given the huge demands for more and more personnel. At the same time, it became clear that those officers assigned to Iraq generally spent an entire year on the embassy compound inside the Green Zone, and hence never saw Iraq or met Iraqis.

In any event, our newly designated ambassador to the U.S. mission to the United Nations in Vienna, James Cunningham, contacted me out of the blue and asked if I was interested in serving as his deputy chief of mission in Vienna. Though I knew little of U.N. work in Vienna, I knew just as little of Iraq. I accepted the Vienna job. Unfortunately, the ambassador was subsequently not confirmed by the Senate, due to Senate policy differences with the State Department on our policy toward the Comprehensive Nuclear Test Ban Treaty Organization in Vienna. Hence, I found myself as chargé d'affairs, running our mission to the United Nations for a year.

The primary and all-consuming challenge was the Iran nuclear issue. In 2002, the Iranians had been caught conducting undeclared—hence, illegal—nuclear activity. In 2003, the Vienna-based International Atomic Energy Agency (IAEA) began investigating as Iran was a signatory to the Non-Proliferation Treaty and had a full-scope Safeguards Agreement with the IAEA. The IAEA discovered during 2003–2004 that Iran was beginning to convert yellowcake uranium, at a facility in Esfahan, into uranium hexafluoride gas, which is subsequently introduced into high-speed centrifuges to produce enriched uranium. In addition, the Iranians were also discovered building an enormous underground facility in Natanz to house thousands of centrifuges for just this purpose. Because centrifuges could be used to produce both low-enriched uranium (LEU) for power plants and medical equipment, as well as highly enriched uranium (HEU) for nuclear weapons, Iran came to represent a central security challenge. The IAEA Board of Governors deployed inspectors increasingly to Iran to catalogue, in its quarterly reports, what the Iranians were up to. Those reports described from 2003 to 2005 the detailed development of the Iranian program.

In mid-2004, at my arrival, the United Kingdom, France, and Germany (referred to as the EU-3) were engaging in direct talks with the Iranians, seeking some kind of agreement to get the

Iranians to stand down from their nuclear efforts and to provide to the IAEA full rights to inspect any and all nuclear facilities. Hassan Rouhani (later elected president of Iran, in 2013) was the chief Iranian negotiator in those years. The United States was anything but sanguine that the EU-3 could achieve much in their talks with Iran, but we tolerated those talks given that we had no diplomatic relations with Iran.

U.S. Ambassador Jackie Wolcott, a political appointee from the Conference on Disarmament in Geneva, would visit Vienna for brief periods to lead formal efforts during quarterly IAEA Board of Governors meetings. Otherwise most of my efforts—and of the entire mission—revolved around getting Iran to stop. I met constantly with the EU-3 ambassadors in Vienna to be briefed on the progress of their talks with Iran, and subsequently kept Washington apprised. On November 15, 2004, the EU-3 governments actually signed the "Paris Agreement" with Iran, which, in effect, committed Iran to "suspend" all of its nuclear activities in exchange for general commitments for a long-term trade and economic deal with the European Union and "objective guarantees" that the Iranian nuclear program was peaceful.

It was a significant breakthrough that surprised many in Washington. Though it was a limited success at the time, I recall some members of the EU-3, who had participated in the negotiations, cautioning me privately that the talks with Iran had been extremely difficult, among the most difficult thing any of them had ever done. They described the negotiations as a kind of "rug merchant," back-and-forth negotiation where no detail had been too small to challenge. There had been a lot of heated tempers and battles. Still, a final text had been reached.

Within weeks, the Iranians began to shut down their nuclear operations. They closed their conversion facility at Esfahan, and the IAEA went in and installed security seals on all parts of the production line operation. The IAEA inspectors also inventoried the Iranian yellowcake and uranium hexafluoride stocks. IAEA inspectors were also permitted into the Natanz underground facility to place seals on the centrifuge work, and Iranian cooperation with the IAEA inspection regime improved. There was a slight hope that progress could be made stopping the program.

However, as 2005 rolled around, it seemed that forward momentum was running out of steam in the EU-3 talks with the Iranians. The United States remained skeptical of, and sometimes antagonistic toward, the entire initiative. The EU-3 seemed pleased that the Iranians had stopped their program, but it did not seem that the EU-3 was vigorously following up with the substantial trade and economic cooperation that had been promised to the Iranians. At the same time, the Iranians continually noted that the "suspension" was not necessarily permanent, but depended on further talks and commitments. And at a strategic level, Iranian relations with the West had not improved in atmosphere at all.

During this period, the United States had maintained strict economic and financial sanctions on Iran, and did not closely associate itself with the EU-3 agreement. Undersecretary of State John Bolton was the primary shaper of U.S. policy, and he appeared extremely skeptical of the IAEA in the aftermath of their work in Iraq. Nevertheless, we did not directly oppose the continuation of EU-3 and IAEA talks with Iran, in an effort to halt the Iranian nuclear program. I met with the EU-3 ambassadors every few days to share views on developments and challenge their efforts. I also met weekly alone with Mohammed ElBaradei, at the time the director general of the IAEA, who was working hard to support the EU-3/Iranian agreement. But 2005 was an election year in Iran, and the Iranian nuclear program fueled sharp controversy during the internal political campaign. It seemed that the nuclear program was being cast as the embodiment of national honor for Iran, something that could not be abandoned or even suspended.

In early August 2005, Mahmoud Ahmadinejad was elected president of Iran. And, finally, about a week later—and almost ten months after the initial agreement—the EU-3 made generalized suggestions for long-term political and economic cooperation with Iran, in exchange for abandonment of work on the nuclear fuel cycle. I had the sense the offer was too late and ill-defined, but rather rushed to presentation after the unexpected election outcome. The new Iranian president immediately rejected the proposal out of hand. Instead of engaging in talks with the EU-3, Iran proceeded within weeks to cut IAEA seals at their conversion facility at Esfahan and began feeding 37 tons of yellowcake uranium into the processing machinery. They broadcast this action on national television. This signaled the end of Iranian adherence to the Paris Agreement, which had survived less than a year.

This Iranian action precipitated a collapse of confidence in Iran and was the catalyst for an emergency IAEA Board of Governors meeting in August, followed by a formal finding by the Board of Governors in September 2005 of Iran being in non-compliance with its safeguards obligations, and another call on Iran to suspend its enrichment-related activities. The resolution also found that Iran's activities gave rise to questions for the U.N. Security

Council, as the organ bearing main responsibility for the maintenance of international peace and security. The resolution established that the Board of Governors would report Iran to the U.N. Security Council at a time of its choosing. This was a momentous finding, with countries from all regions of the world supporting the decision, though a significant number sided with Iran.

Unfortunately, Iran did not respond constructively. Rather, on January 3, 2006, Iran announced to the IAEA that it was cutting all of the seals at the enrichment facility at Natanz and starting up its centrifuges. Enrichment would resume. I summoned the Russian, French, British, German, and Chinese ambassadors together in January 2006, to find a way to collectively protest this action to the Iranians. I had spent some months courting the Russian and Chinese ambassadors, in particular, as they were crucial for our efforts to get anything done. After some debate, we all agreed to protest the matter in the same terms to Iran. The solidarity with the EU-3, and China and Russia, was striking and took the Iranians aback. It was the only time up to and probably after that point that the five permanent members of the Security Council protested in the same words to Iran. We know it caught the Iranians' attention.

In addition, the Iranian action led to an emergency meeting of the IAEA Board of Governors, February 2–4, 2006, which resulted in a decision to report Iran formally to the U.N. Security Council. In that decision, the board also called on Iran to immediately reestablish full suspension of all enrichment-related and reprocessing activities; halt construction of the heavy-water reactor; ratify and implement the Additional Protocol; and implement transparency measures. That remained the agenda for the next decade. This was all extremely hard-fought diplomacy, fighting for every vote against Iran.

European and other countries were extremely frustrated during these years with the unwillingness of the United States to speak directly to the Iranians, who had a large delegation in Vienna. Iran and the United States would be present at Board of Governors meetings, and each would speak to the plenary. However, we avoided any direct contact, even in the elevators. In March 2005, the British ambassador invited me to a dinner with two dozen other ambassadors, at his home. He cautioned that the Iranian ambassador would also be present, but he pledged to seat me far from the Iranian. After consulting with Washington, which was not pleased, I attended the dinner anyway. I shook hands with Iranian Ambassador Ali Akbar Salehi, who was a rather quiet and subdued individual. He was not known for ideological outbursts. He later lost his job after Ahmadinejad came to power, but a few years later became Iranian foreign minister. At the dinner he offered a greeting, but there was no substantive exchange.

After 2006 the political action on Iran moved largely to the U.N. Security Council in New York. The United Nations imposed several sets of sanctions during the years Ahmadinejad was in power. The same years were accompanied by a dramatic increase in the nuclear program activity. I told ElBaradei during this time that it was probably impossible to deal with Ahmadinejad, and we have to just wait him out. I truly believed Ahmadinejad was irrational and unwilling to engage in substance on this issue. Unless we desired war, we would have to wait for his successor.

In the summer of 2005, Mohammed ElBaradei was up for

reelection as director general of the IAEA. He was extremely controversial in Washington. Some believed he was overly accommodating to Iran. Others believed he was performing well. During the year leading up to his reelection, consideration was given to a variety of other possible candidates for the position, while at the same time we were pressing him to pressure Iran. By late spring 2005, the group of G-77 developing countries summoned

INTERNATIONAL ATOMIC ENERGY AGENCY DIRECTOR GENERAL MOHAMMED ELBARADEI AND THE AUTHOR IN VIENNA 2007

me to a meeting in Vienna to state to me formally their unconditional support for ElBaradei's reelection. This was the largest bloc of votes in the IAEA membership. After this, the Europeans and other countries, one by one, began to approach me, to quietly state their support for ElBaradei and urge U.S. support as well. Washington was not happy.

Suddenly, in early summer 2005, ElBaradei was invited to Washington to meet with Secretary Rice and others. I was told to make the trip happen. I spent a long discussion utilizing every skill in persuasion I had to convince ElBaradei to make the trip. He was well aware that he had detractors in Washington, and that Washington opposed him. But in the end he decided to go. He was subsequently reelected for another term, with U.S. support. Several months later he was awarded the Nobel Peace Prize. From my private discussions with him, I came away with the impression that he was a brilliant statesman and diplomat, who mastered nuance and discretion but suffered from the intractable nature in those days of the Washington-Tehran standoff.

One of Washington's higher priorities in 2004–2005 was to also get the IAEA general membership of some 144 countries to agree to create a new "Safeguards Committee" to focus member states more directly on nuclear safeguards issues (code words for Iran nuclear infractions). Many countries opposed this idea, especially since it was a U.S. proposal. They believed it was a U.S. ploy to corner Iran. In addition, the United States was not viewed internationally as neutral on any issues, and therefore should be opposed. I worked diligently during a year to convince, cajole, persuade, encourage, and shove country ambassadors to accept the proposal and ignore the origin of the idea. I argued the importance of looking harder at nuclear safeguards in a world of growing globalization and proliferation. It was a tough battle.

After negotiating a variety of changes to the proposal over several months, I managed to have sufficient support to get the proposal considered in plenary in June 2005. I had to phone ElBaradei almost daily to ensure his sometimes-wobbly support of the proposal. On the day before the vote, I asked one of my officers, Jeff Dubel, to approach every single ambassador in the meeting hall to arrange brief, eyeball-to-eyeball side chats with me. I pressed them, one by one, in firmest language, for votes in support of the resolution. I phoned several foreign ministries directly, including China, pressing for support. The vote surprised many. It carried unanimously with one exception: Iran abstained. I had managed for the first time to isolate Iran on a major vote in the IAEA, and everyone had noticed. Iran was stung. A modest achievement at the time that was credited by the White House. Most moving to me was a small handwritten note passed to me by a retiring officer, Jim Hamilton, which read, "This would not have happened without you." A modest treasure from one of the State Department's top nuclear experts. I was subsequently promoted to minister-counselor, equivalent to a two-star general. Within a year, I was offered the position of ambassador to Kazakhstan, which I had to decline.

L TO R: GEORGE GLASS, RUSSIAN AMBASSADOR, KUWAITI AMBASSADOR, BRITISH AMBASSADOR PETER JENKINS, INDIAN AMBASSADOR SHARMA, LEBANESE AMBASSADOR, OMANI AMBASSADOR, IRAQI AMBASSADOR AT HOME OF KUWAITI AMBASSADOR IN VIENNA 2006

It would have required me sending my children back to the United States to finish high school on their own. The timing was bad, and family came first.

In late summer 2005, Washington sent Ambassador Greg Schulte to run the mission, and I remained as deputy chief of mission until mid-2007. During that period, the Iran issue continued to dominate the agenda. Schulte was tough and abrasive on the

Iran issue. He pushed relentlessly to corral votes. He was a career government official, and his passion and conviction were critical to forcing some members of the Board of Governors to refer Iran to the Security Council in 2006. Schulte deployed brute diplomatic force where I relied on quieter persuasion. He was later criticized by Washington inspectors for being tough with his staff, but he deserves substantial credit for achieving some tough votes in Vienna. Being nice has never been sufficient, in itself, to get results in international forays.

Indeed, diplomacy can be scary. At one point in 2006, the ambassador of a significant country in Asia approached me to share that the Iranians were directly threatening to cancel several major construction projects in his country if he voted against Iran in an upcoming resolution. The ambassador was terrified and unsure of what to do. Another critical ambassador from a country allied with the United States revealed a series of similar threats against that country's financial sector. That ambassador shrugged them off, although the act of sharing the threats with me revealed a deeper concern about how serious things were getting. A third ambassador from a major North African country approached me as well to share that the president of the ambassador's country had received a phone call from Ahmadinejad complaining about the voting demeanor of that specific ambassador. The ambassador was fearful of being fired because Iran was upset. Also, I heard repeatedly that when G-77 meetings of many developing countries took place, if anyone even hinted at a position at odds with Iran, the speaker was immediately shouted down and vilified by Iranian diplomats. Many diplomats seemed outright fearful to be in Iran's sights. These were unusual anecdotes, which nonetheless underscore the hardball nature of dealing with issues related to Iran in those years.

I spent a good deal of effort on other battlefronts. The Egyptian ambassador consistently worked to win support for a nuclear-free zone in the Middle East, an idea that sounds attractive at one level—until the Israelis are considered. This annual effort each fall aggravated Washington and Israel profoundly. It resulted in rather dramatic votes at the annual IAEA General Conference, but had little actual effect. For some, the idea was a convenient ploy to distract countries from the specific Iran program.

In early 2007, Secretary Rice visited Vienna for a meeting with the Europeans. I met her briefly. Rice had committed to "transformational diplomacy," which meant using any possible means to deploy large numbers of diplomats to

THE AUTHOR AND SECRETARY OF STATE CONDOLEEZZA RICE IN VIENNA IN MAY 2007

populous countries like China, India, and Nigeria, if not Iraq. People were being transferred in large numbers out of key countries like Germany, France, the United Kingdom, and Japan, and deployed to the developing world, which reflected a shift of priorities away from the developed world. I did not comprehend this at all. In any event, the Department had turned decidedly against family-friendliness after the departure of Colin Powell. Indeed, the director general of the Foreign Service phoned me personally to urge me to go to Iraq for a year, without my family, a year when all hell was breaking loose. I could not envision a constructive role to be played there at that time beyond mere survival, and I had already burned my family once. I moved on to Colorado Springs and my children nonetheless paid a very heavy price for their most disruptive high school transfers.

CHAPTER SEVENTEEN

COLORADO: NORAD/NORTHCOM

(2007)

I was reluctant to return to Washington, which tended to impoverish my family during each tour. This became even more challenging with two children in high school. So I accepted the offer of political advisor at NORAD-NORTH-COM, in Colorado Springs. We moved there and bought a small house in mid-2007. I had never worked at a military base before, so it promised to be a change.

Colorado was a tough adjustment for the kids. First impressions were lasting, and my children quickly obtained the impression that everyone in the area was either carrying guns or bibles, or both. Stop signs were adorned with bullet holes, and church services seemed exclusively evangelical in nature. The amount of gun violence was stunning. The high school was academically underwhelming, and promised little assistance with looming college admissions. The grades of both my children immediately plummeted. High school acquaintances of my daughter were shot at one point; other friends were arrested. Our house was in a gated community, which I came to appreciate. Local residents had little knowledge of, or interest in, foreign affairs.

However, NORAD-NORTHCOM, one of only nine major military commands, was impressive. I worked as an adviser to four-star commander Victor Renuart, on foreign affairs aspects of NORAD-NORTHCOM operations. It was an undefined position, which nonetheless came with a motivated staff and generous military support. I was permitted to meddle wherever I wished, and provide commentary directly to the commander on any findings. I loved it.

During my two years, I accompanied Renuart on trips to Australia, Mexico City, the Arctic Circle, London, Brussels, Naples, Reykjavik,

NORAD-NORTHCOM COMMANDER VICTOR E. "GENE" RENUART & STATE DEPARTMENT POLITICAL ADVISOR GEORGE GLASS IN COLORADO 2009

Ottawa, Nassau, and Miami. These were usually aboard a military Gulfstream V, which was the most efficient and comfortable mode of travel I have ever encountered. I learned that, since 9/11, all combatant commanders had to travel via such military jets because Washington required that they could be reached every hour of the day. Because NORTHCOM was responsible for protecting North America from any attack, our commander was always on call. I traveled to Washington with the commander every few weeks. During those trips, I would visit different offices around the State

Department or the National Security Council to ferret out what was happening on key foreign policy issues. It was a great opportunity to see colleagues in various parts of the foreign policy world. I would subsequently share those foreign policy insights with the commander, laced with my own comments, which allowed him to focus his attention solely on military matters at the Pentagon.

One of NORTHCOM's primary responsibilities was dealing with North American disasters such as Hurricane Katrina, which I thankfully missed. The command was frequently asked to support relief efforts from hurricanes and wildfires all around the country. These events generally did not affect foreign affairs, or my role, unless they crossed into Mexico or Canada. Occasionally this was the case, as when we helped to provide flood relief in Mexico. However, the command was routinely assisting FEMA and state governments during hurricanes and forest fires, bringing military assets to each crisis. Indeed, the intertwining with a military combatant command with a multitude of Washington agencies and local agencies seemed to betray a growing trend in the military. Rather than work interagency issues in Washington, bring the interagency representatives to your command, such as in Colorado, where you can manage them. At least for disaster relief it seemed to have some merit. But it was not of great personal interest to me.

NORTHCOM had a particular role in strategic deterrence and missile defense, given its underground command and control assets in Cheyenne Mountain. Participation in regular military exercises of strategic operations was intriguing. It was big-league war gaming, thinking the unthinkable, and being prepared. I also spent a certain amount of time reflecting on and debating the prospects and challenges to U.S. missile defense efforts around the

PRESIDENTIAL CANDIDATE BARACK OBAMA VISITS NORAD-
NORTHCOM IN JULY 2008

world. There was some internal skepticism of the utility of U.S. missile defense plans in Europe, which were ostensibly designed to stop Iranian missiles. Some insiders noted that stopping a missile from Iran to Europe only provided seconds to make a decision on launching interceptors. This was much more challenging than decision-making on missiles flying across the Atlantic or Pacific. However, missile defense of Europe fell to NATO, not NORAD. My sense was that the politics of having some kind of real defense was politically essential. Still, there was solid conviction that

NORAD-NORTHCOM missile defense of North America was realistic and functional.

Indeed, when North Korean once launched a missile toward Hawaii, the command stood up in preparation to take action to counter the missile if necessary. I sat with the commander, with an open phone to the deputy secretary of state, in the event of problems. The North Korean missile flight was unsuccessful. At another time, the command was used to help shoot down a satellite that had fallen from orbit and was threatening damage if it entered the atmosphere. It was a successful action. The discussions of missile defense and its limitations were stimulating and

NORAD-NORTHCOM POLITICAL ADVISOR GLASS WELCOMES VISITING STATE DEPARTMENT DEPUTY ASSISTANT SECRETARY KEVIN O'KEEFE IN JANUARY 2008

sobering, and even though the defense was ostensibly designed against Iranian and North Korean threats, I could not always shake the Cold War visions of Soviet ICBMs landing. Perhaps a matter of too much Dr. Strangelove.

NORTHCOM's geographic responsibility for North America

included Mexico. This permitted several trips to Mexico City to meet with the defense minister and other officials. Discussion from the U.S. side tended to focus on efforts to combat narcotics trafficking from Mexico to the United States. The Mexicans, however, complained routinely about the flood of weapons out of the United States to Mexico, demanding U.S. action to stop them. It was an exchange of views that persisted but never seemed to progress.

Another key issue at NORAD-NORTHCOM was Russia. Moscow was regularly dispatching Bear bombers over the Arctic to the Canadian or U.S. borders, even though the Cold War had ended years earlier. It reminded me of Japan. The planes would approach Canada directly, and then turn onto other trajectories just at the edge of Canadian airspace. However, we would frequently scramble planes to intercept, just in case they did not turn. It was a strange cat-and-mouse game that became more dramatic at times when international tensions increased, such as during the 2008 Georgian crisis. That said, the command worked hard to establish direct contacts with the counterpart Russian strategic command. Visits had taken place in earlier years, and we were on the verge of achieving a new round of visits in early 2008. But the Georgia crisis stopped cold any new round of contacts. During the 2008 Russia-Georgia crisis, there was a distinct whiff of the Cold War, even in Colorado Springs. I was struck by the resounding military support for taking resolute action to support Georgia. We were ready to act, but I was skeptical that military action on our part was advisable.

The melting Arctic ice cap was also a growing concern in Colorado Springs. It presaged a dramatic upturn in competition for resources in the Arctic, as well as ship and other traffic through the Arctic. Given the harsh conditions and difficulty in providing any rescue assistance, the number of ships that got into trouble in the Arctic would certainly increase. NORTHCOM would increasingly be drawn into responding to emergency requests in the Arctic as the ice receded.

Moreover, because the United States had not yet signed the Convention on the Law of Sea, its own claims to the Arctic would come into question soon. Different parts of the command studied this

NORAD-NORTHCOM POLITICAL ADVISOR GLASS (RED HAT) IN INUVIK, NORTHERN TERRITORIES VISITING WITH CANADIAN ESKIMO RANGERS IN 2009

issue, but were unable to change much. Congress did not appear ready to accept any U.N. role in any Convention on the Law of the Sea. And the United States had no funds for new icebreakers or Arctic bases.

Counterterrorism was a chief responsibility of the command. A significant effort was devoted to domestic coordination in the event of an attack of any kind. The command enjoyed the presence of at least one liaison officer from each counterterrorism-related domestic agency in Washington. This facilitated preparations and communications for responding to any contingency. On several occasions the command dispatched fighter jets to intercept irregular flight violations of restricted airspace. When the Democratic National Convention came to Denver and the Winter Olympic Games came to Vancouver, NORTHCOM was a primary provider of ground and air security for such events.

Spies Again

Every now and then throughout my career, intelligence cases would pop up, and always unexpectedly. Even in distant Colorado, this happened yet again. On June 4, 2009, the press reported that Kendall Myers and his wife had been arrested and indicted for espionage. History surprised me yet again: Kendall Myers had been a professor of mine in 1975, while I was attending the Johns Hopkins School of Advanced International Studies, in Washington. He had taught modern German politics with no noticeable political agenda. When I joined the State Department in 1981, I attended regional training about Germany at the Foreign Service Institute for two weeks, where I found Kendall Myers again as an instructor on German affairs. He subsequently became the Department of State's expert on German affairs inside the Bureau of Intelligence and Research for many years. Myers and his wife were sentenced to life in prison for espionage. They had been spying for Cuba. Such reports always took my breath away.

NORAD-NORTHCOM was a well-run command, with truly magnificent leaders. However, it was almost completely a "planning" headquarters, with some 2,000 people dedicated solely to making plans for various contingencies. When it needed "assets" to deploy on a mission, it had to ask the Pentagon to assign such assets (e.g., ships, planes) for deployment. I used to jokingly ask the commander where the bottled water and blankets were waiting for the next emergency.

I was awed by the resources that the military had at its disposal. I was advised that I had funds for travel wherever and whenever I needed to go anywhere in the world. Indeed, I was encouraged once to fly to Manila for the sole purpose of a brief chat with our ambassador. I did not go. Most of the twenty-plus generals at the command were traveling every week. This contrasted substantially with the State Department, where travel money was extremely restricted my entire career, and our senior leaders rarely had military planes to utilize.

I was invited to remain a third year at NORAD-NORTH-COM, but I declined. I wanted to try to get my son into a high school somewhere else that would boost his college application efforts in a year. After that, I did not care. Berlin had respected international schools that would help, if I could manage another year there. My daughter had graduated high school in Colorado Springs after a tumultuous experience. I owed my son a try.

CHAPTER EIGHTEEN

BERLIN FAREWELL

(2009)

Early in the summer of 2009, the European bureau phoned to ask if I would be willing to travel to Berlin and run the embassy as chargé d'affaires, and then as deputy chief of mission, once a new ambassador was confirmed. They said I was best equipped.. I noted that I would need a few weeks to prepare for the move. However, time ran out. Within days a new ambassador was being announced by the White House, and he chose a deputy without considering my interest. Though not particularly challenging position, I agreed to go to Berlin anyway as minister-counselor of political affairs, in August 2009. It would be good for the family and for my son's last year of high school, and fun to see how the city had changed since unification.

September 2009 included German national elections. These provided a nice reintroduction for me to German politics and more traditional diplomatic work. I attended FDP party conventions, where Guido Westerwelle seemed unstoppable on his road to foreign minister. Though nary a mention of foreign affairs could be found in his campaign speeches, he was a dramatic and forceful speaker. I knew from earlier observations that Chancellor Angela Merkel would also be a most formidable force. The embassy reporting of the elections was highly praised.

The assignment was second nature, but it was refreshing to see many old friends. Throughout these two years, the key issue was the European financial crisis, sovereign debt, and Greece. Though economic in nature, the solutions and ideas were largely political. The political section made a substantial effort to sort out the party differences and decipher Berlin's financial policy for Washington. As the Bundestag wrestled with different initiatives on stabilizing the Euro and Greece, I would phone the various party caucuses for updates on positions, and provide detailed reporting to Washington. Our team of political officers developed incredible access to all of the political parties. We were trusted. We asked piercing questions. We could get to see any German officials. This was the bread and butter of diplomatic work.

I worked hard to emphasize the special nature of the German relationship with the United States. However, I had the impression there was little resonance on this count in Washington. This became a growing source of frustration. Germany seemed to be the single most powerful country on the continent, yet absolutely no U.S. senators or congressmen ever visited the country. In addition, we rarely ever entertained visits by U.S. cabinet members. I had the distinct impression that Germany was of little interest to Washington. Indeed, even when the Euro crisis was threatening the unity of Europe, and Greeks were marching in the streets comparing German austerity to Hitlerism, Washington seemed to barely notice. I emphasized in reporting and presentations that Germany was central to U.S. influence on the continent, and that the transatlantic alliance had been built by the United States. We could not just ignore it. Washington's reaction was one of simply asking what more Germany could do to help in Afghanistan. I was again speechless.

WikiLeaks

By late 2010 the WikiLeaks crisis erupted in a big way. A substantial amount of the embassy's alleged reporting became searchable online. Many of our closest contacts on Chancellor Merkel's staff, in the political parties, or at the top echelons of the Foreign Office, could be found candidly evaluating our views of German policy in our reports. Some were mildly critical of individual German leaders, and this caused some consternation when we allegedly quoted them. Some of our contacts who were identified may have had their careers damaged. In any event, WikiLeaks substantially destroyed our credibility and ability to work as political officers. Governments will not admit such damage between allies, but there could have been no other result, given the circumstances. Grave damage was done.

One leaked report described how a young German politician, Helmut Metzner, working for the FDP, shared with the embassy his insights into the coalition-building negotiations that ensued in the wake of the 2009 German elections. Such negotiations were politically interesting but hardly earth-shattering outside of Germany. In the report, the drafting officer had not actually named Metzner, but simply referred to him as a reliable source with a promising future. That reference, however, set off a front-page search in Germany for the "mole" who was "reporting" to the U.S. embassy in Berlin. It smelled of Cold War tactics, when it was in fact nothing of significance. The scandal plagued German primetime news for two solid weeks, until the German FDP uncovered the person as the FDP office director of Foreign Minister Guido Westerwelle. The person was immediately fired and pilloried in the press as a quasi-traitor. Though he was investigated by German law enforcement, he was subsequently exonerated of any wrongdoing. Indeed, his job working for Westerwelle had included designated responsibility for "international" contacts. Such positions routinely entailed briefing foreign diplomats on what was going on in the FDP. But politics has its own paradigm, and WikiLeaks directly destroyed his career in front of 80 million German TV viewers. I watched with profound sadness, unable to rescue decades of German trust that had suddenly gone up in smoke.

After that, it was impossible for the embassy to have open discussions or obtain reliable political reporting. Of course neither Washington nor the Germans wanted to hear such blasphemy. But it was inescapable. I would call on German parliamentarians, and they would bring in their own note-takers to record everything that was said (including by me), in order to avoid anything less than completely benign platitudes. I was never able to have another interesting conversation after WikiLeaks. Washington did not seem concerned, but then it seemed disinclined to rely on or digest diplomatic reporting anyway. I urged Washington to consider assigning several new, young officers to Berlin in order to begin a multi-year process of building a new generation of contacts. My appeals gained no traction whatsoever, as Washington was into cutting budgets, not expanding staff. Within several months, inspectors came to Berlin and actually forced the political section to downsize and cut positions. There seemed to be no more interest in what was really happening on the German political scene. Between WikiLeaks and the inspectors, it seemed that Washington was losing interest in what had been, in my view, the most important U.S. ally and anchor of stability in continental Europe. This seemed to be borne out even more by the new ballyhooed pivot to Asia.

Afghanistan

Occasionally other foreign policy issues would pass through Berlin. On one occasion, leading members of the Afghanistan Northern Alliance visited Berlin in order to meet with a small group of U.S. congressmen. I wound up briefing the congressmen and accompanying them to a lengthy dinner with the Afghans. It was a stimulating dinner, which allowed me several lengthy side exchanges with the Afghans. They described to me multitudes of unlimited arsenals of guns at their disposal in Afghanistan. They said they could mobilize 100,000 people if necessary. They sharply criticized the Karzai government and the recent U.S. approach to Afghanistan. It was a most colorful discussion from a world away. It reminded me of my work on Bosnia and Iran, and the many interlocutors who had been totally indecipherable.

Philip Murphy was the ambassador during this time in Germany. He was a tremendously gregarious and friendly interlocutor. Coming from the financial world, he was interested in the Euro crisis, but worked hard to ensure every task. His official dinners for various collections of German guests were renowned for their style and charm. He prepared like no other ambassador, delivering at least one question to each specific guest to ensure broad participation. He was the perfect host and networker. But did it matter in Washington? I felt that Washington was further from Berlin than ever in my career.

From time to time I would look up various German personalities from earlier times in Germany. At one point, I invited former East German interior minister Peter-Michael Diestel to lunch. We had not met since our lunch in 1990, around the time of unification. Diestel was now working as a lawyer, but claimed to have extensive contacts, still, to the old regime. He said that his strength had been that the old communists and Stasi had trusted him. I told him that when we had last met in 1990, I had been wondering privately whether he was planning a coup against the de Maizière government, as some had feared. Diestel looked at me and said that, yes, he could have succeeded in taking over the government; he had thought about it. It had been possible, given his credible standing with the security services. However, he also told me that Chancellor Kohl had extracted a promise from him to see unification through as planned. Diestel claimed he had decided to comply.

On another occasion, I had lunch with Joachim Gauck, formerly a Lutheran pastor from Rostock and the first Federal Commissioner for the Stasi Records. Gauck arrived alone, and on foot, a display of the profound humbleness that I had always detected around him. The meeting entailed a wide-ranging and open discussion of politics and foreign affairs in Germany. Gauck professed extreme interest in the United States, about which he claimed to know little. He was one of the most personable individuals I have ever met, and the very embodiment of morality and integrity. He offered to meet again. Several months later, he became president of Germany.

On another occasion, I participated in a breakfast meeting of Secretary of State Hillary Clinton and German Chancellor Angela Merkel. As I was gazing out the window of the chancellor's office, she came up from behind, tapped me on the shoulder, and introduced herself to me. I was shocked by such graciousness. The breakfast meeting covered a wide range of issues, from European debt to the Middle East. The Merkel-Clinton exchange was riveting and substantive from start to finish. These were two of the smartest people to be found anywhere.

Germany's Anniversary

One of the most moving events I engineered was a 20th anniversary party in late 2010 for key members of the last East German government, the only one to have been freely elected. Attendees included former prime minister Lothar de Maizière, former defense minister Rainer Eppelman, former president Sabine Bergman-Pohl, as well as key figures from the parliament. Former U.S. ambassador Richard Barkley also attended. I hosted the event at the embassy on Pariser Platz, which none of these individuals had ever visited. I adorned the event with a chocolate "birthday cake" to unified Germany, but we did not sing. Discussion was focused on the events of 1989–1990, and what really happened. After 20 years, virtually none of those who had brought about unification had any role in modern German politics. However, their praise of U.S. leadership and support for unification was nothing short of overwhelming. No country, they resounded, did more for Germany than the United States.

LUNCH FOR FORMER EAST GERMAN LEADERS L TO R: GUENTER NOOKE, RAINER EPPELMAN, U.S. AMBASSADOR RICHARD BARKLEY, LOTHAR DE MAIZIERE, GEORGE GLASS IN U.S. EMBASSY BERLIN ON SEPTEMBER 29, 2010

I decided to leave the Service after two years in Berlin. My son had a good year in school in Berlin before being accepted to university. Berlin had always been a central focus of my political life, even before joining the government. It was the appropriate place to depart after thirty-one years in government.

During my final days, I emphasized to the ambassador and senior staff that, of all things, we must grow ears again. We, both in Berlin and Washington, needed to listen to the world and try to understand the different views of others. We were too busy spouting off talking points, time and time and time again, as if the more we stated our position on things the more persuasive we would be.

"parrott-speak" reinforced by the blaring Internet, was neither understanding nor persuasion. It was simply advertising. This was not working. Measuring diplomatic effectiveness by page views of a Twitter message by the State Department was not diplomacy, nor was it persuasion. It would bear no fruit. Wearing a

GEORGE GLASS WITH U.S. AMBASSADOR PHILIP MURPHY ATOP THE U.S. EMBASSY IN BERLIN 2011

foreign policy on one's forehead was disingenuous and precluded any negotiation from the start. Indeed, only diplomatic ambiguity permitted drawing out foreign leaders to test their flexibility, and possibly seeking common ground with them.

My father's generation had devoted their best minds to devising a peaceful and prosperous postwar world, founded on the German anchor in Europe and the Japanese anchor in Asia. They created the United Nations, Bretton Woods, and the financial institutions that served fairly well for decades and that ensured a leading and determinant role for the United States. Their concept was brimming not only with freedom and democracy, but also with tolerance and understanding. It would, I argued, be myopic to jettison such a world without any notion of what was to replace it. I had heard no talk of vision or concept since the days of Warren Christopher. Where were we going? Why were we closing our consulates in Germany and reducing our diplomatic presence when Germany was leading Europe? In the early 1980s, German young people attacked me relentlessly on U.S. policy. But now, when I spoke to them, it was as if they were tuned out and apathetic. They were starting not to care anymore. The storms of history had left Germany, but should we be leaving too? The greatest achievement of my father's generation had been building the greatest of allies out of the greatest of enemies. That was not a cookie-cutter exercise that would necessarily apply elsewhere today, but it should also not be cast aside as yesterday's world without relevance.

CHAPTER NINETEEN

AFTERWORD

My wife and I moved to Garmisch-Parten-kirchen upon my leaving the Service. My Washington Monument and Duck Pond are far away, and I am left contemplating mountains shimmering in the distant mist. I have never been more convinced of the importance of diplomacy than now, nor more terrified of the threats the nation faces. There is nothing, absolutely nothing that can come close to looking a foreigner in the eye and connecting via humanness, despite challenging cultures and political systems. Arguments that email and phones obviate the need for diplomacy are simply unwilling to embrace the challenge of building on human ingenuity and connection.

It is frightening to look in the eyes of someone who may be a mass murderer, or someone who is probably skimming millions from his government. But it is far easier to extract marginal progress around an issue, in person, than receiving flat rejections or silence to our messages. The world cannot be managed from the phone or email of one person in Washington. Relying on news reporting to tell us what a country or a government is about is superficial and riddled with perils of overreaction. It is only the diplomats who peer into the eyes of other worlds, seek to fathom meaning, and report the significance for U.S. interests. More and more diplomats are allowing themselves to be chained to computers, mistaking emails or news blurbs for exploration of tomorrow's allies. This can only lead to isolationism and pitfalls.

The debate will continue to rage over the value of having virtually every U.S. ambassador posted to Europe and Japan lacking any particular credentials beyond campaign assistance. I have enjoyed in many ways virtually every ambassador I ever worked for. However, I have never detected value that merited recruiting outside of the Foreign Service. I have never seen a political appointee achieve policy changes unless forced on him by circumstance. I have never seen one write an evaluation of, or award nomination for, a Foreign Service employee. I have seen them spend all their time building their own networks, which they all hoped secretly to later utilize in their post-diplomatic endeavors. I have seen them repeatedly decline to share experiences from their past non-diplomatic lives regardless of how interested their staff was. Yet we were expected to be open books to whatever they desired. They were uniformly surprised by the normal challenges that come to every embassy, and all but unwilling, if not downright fearful, to hear bad news. Yet I liked, respected, and enjoyed every one of them. Yet being nice is not enough on the front lines. Every person has shortcomings, but to suppress the full potential of diplomacy in Europe and Asia in critical places by utilizing non-career persons is not in the national interest.

I wish to watch my ducklings under the shadow of the Washington Monument. I wish to relive my own profound beliefs in freedom, individualism, entrepreneurship, tolerance, due process, and the pursuit of happiness. I hope my ducklings are still there when I have the chance to drop by.

ACKNOWLDGEMENTS

I would like to thank my friend Jon Eaton for his guidance and direction developing this manuscript. Jane W. Cormuss provided invaluable copy editing assistance. Foreign Service Officer Chad Peterson reviewed the text and provided substantive input to draw out various policy points. Inspiration and encouragement for the work was drawn from the inquisitive discussions and encouragement over the years from JCK, KG, CD, JR, JAS, AB, NG, MG, and countless others, not least my loyal friend Georgene Becker and my grandfather George Edgar Hamilton. They were more helpful and encouraging than imaginable. Thank you. This work is a portrayal of the way I saw things as a witness to history, which by nature must be subjective. Errors of fact or interpretation are mine alone.

138	EDMOND STOIBER	1999 Bayerische Staatskanzlei (Bavarian State Government)
139	GEORGE TENET	1997 U.S. Consulate Munich, Department of State
141	WILLIAM COHEN/CARL LEVIN	1998 Department of Dffense
142	WILLIAM COHEN/JOHN KORNBLUM	1998 Department of Defense
156	WAYNE-NEWCOMB	2004 Department of State
180	MOHAMMED ELBARADEI	2007 U.S. Mission Vienna, Department of State
182	KUWAITI AMBASSADOR	2006 U.S. Mission Vienna, Department of State
184	CONDOLEEZZA RICE	2007 Department of State
188	VICTOR E. RENUART	2009 Norad-Northcom, Department of Defense
190	BARACK OBAMA	2008 Norad-Northcom, Department of Defense
191	NORTHCOM WELCOME	2008 Norad-Northcom, Department of Defense
193	RIFLE TRAINING	2009 Norad-Northcom, Department of Defense
204	GERMANY ANNIVERSARY	2010 U.S. Embassy Berlin, Department of State
205	PHILIP MURPHY	2010 U.S. Embassy Berlin, Department of State
211	BRANDENBURG GATE ICON	© Can Stock Photo Inc. / grum
BACK COVER	DUCK POND	© 2014 Nicole Glass

www.ingramcontent.com/pod-product-compliance
Lightning Source LLC
Chambersburg PA
CBHW040255100426
42811CB00011B/1266